The Holistic Nutritionist's Guide to Lawful Practice in Canada

Glenn M. Rumbell, B.A., LL.B.

© 2011
The Canadian Association of Natural Nutritional Practitioners
(CANNP)

All rights reserved. No part of this book may be reproduced, stored in a retrieval system or transmitted in any form or by any means, electronic, mechanical, photocopying, recording or otherwise without the prior written permission of the publisher.

This publication is not engaged in providing legal or other professional advice. If legal or other expert advice is required, a licensed lawyer or other appropriate professional should be consulted. The analysis contained within this book represents the viewpoint of the author and should in no way be construed as being official or unofficial policy of the publisher or any governmental body.

Canadian Cataloguing in Publication Data

Rumbell, Glenn M.
The Holistic Nutritionist's Guide to Lawful Practice in Canada

ISBN -13: 978-1461150848

Preface

This book was commissioned by the Canadian Association of Natural Nutritional Practitioners (CANNP) in response to a need for a single resource for Holistic Nutritionists across Canada that summarizes the laws surrounding their profession.

The term "Nutritionist" is one of those fuzzy, undefined terms that we use every day and often do not think about. In one sense, its meaning is obvious—a Nutritionist is a person who knows and provides advice about nutritional well-being. But on the other hand, this definition does not tell us much, because in most areas of Canada anyone can call themselves a Nutritionist, regardless of their training, experience, beliefs or manner of practice. And in provinces where its meaning is defined, and where the practice of a Nutritionist is regulated, the "Nutritionists" who practise there are not the ones for whom this book is written.

This book was written for unregulated, unlicensed independent Nutritionists. By this I mean individuals who provide advice about nutrition to clients, but who are not members of a provincially regulated health profession because they have an alternative approach to promoting health and well-being—individuals who view the body holistically. Individuals who believe health is not defined by the absence of disease but rather by the presence of vitality and energy. Individuals who believe natural *is* necessarily better. Nutritionists who believe you truly are what you eat.

The purpose of this book is to provide unlicensed Nutritionists with an understanding of the major regulations that restrict what they can and cannot do in their daily practices and how they represent themselves to the public.

If you are an unlicensed Nutritionist, it is crucially important that you know this. We live in an age of increasing government regulation within the health industry. All too frequently this regulation is centred on protecting consumers by defining government-approved health professions and giving these groups monopolies over whole areas of practice. While the motive may be good (the protection of consumers), the end result can be less so, particularly when there are competing philosophical perspectives on the approach that should be taken to health.

This has led to widely different approaches across Canada to the regulation of health services, ranging from the open door environment of Alberta—where anyone is free to diagnose and treat diseases and disorders (provided that they do not prescribe or administer a treatment that is restricted)—to the closed door world of New Brunswick, where it is illegal for anyone but a licensed Dietitian (or member of another Regulated Health Profession that is similarly empowered) to be provide the service of "assessing nutritional needs of individuals and developing and implementing nutritional care plans based on the assessments."

With a little knowledge and careful organization of your practice you can safely, effectively and profitably operate an unlicensed Nutritionist practice in much of Canada. This book is designed to assist you in so doing.

I would like to thank the many people who assisted in the research and writing of this book, including my fellow directors at the Canadian Association of Natural Nutritional Practitioners, Wendy Gibson and Beth Gorbet, my good friend and business partner, Martin Ross, and the many others within the industry who reviewed and provided comments on this book. Thank you all.

Glenn Rumbell
Toronto,
April 2011

How to Use this Book

This book has been structured to enable readers to quickly and efficiently gain an understanding of the laws in effect in their province.

Chapters 1 and 2 provide a general overview of the regulation of health service practitioners throughout Canada to provide a framework in which the laws of each province can be understood.

Chapter 3 contains summaries of the laws of each province, organized alphabetically on a province by province basis. I have also included extracts from the statutes and regulations that most directly impact unlicensed Nutritionists to allow readers the opportunity to review the actual words that detail what can and cannot be done. After reading chapters 1 and 2, you should carefully review the legislative summary for your province, including these extracts.

Chapter 4 contains a discussion of the meanings of key terms that are used throughout the provincial statutes and regulations, terms such as "diagnose" and "drug" and "practice of Medicine" and "treatment." It is crucial to read this chapter, as it is virtually impossible to know what a prohibition against rendering a diagnosis means, for example, unless one also knows what actions have been found to constitute this activity.

The last chapter of this book is designed to enable the reader to pull everything together. In this section there are concrete recommendations on how to organize and run an unlicensed Nutritional consulting practice in a way that minimizes the chances of breaching the laws of your province.

As you read this book, you will also notice that I have relied upon several stock phrases throughout.

I have chosen to refer to unlicensed Nutritionists as "**Holistic Nutritionists**" to clearly differentiate them from the licensed Nutritionists who exist in some provinces as part of a combined profession of Dietitians and Nutritionists. The phrase "**Regulated Health Professions**" refers collectively to all health professions, (e.g., Dietetics, Medicine, Naturopathy, etc.) that are formally regulated within a province and that require a licence to practice. To simplify matters somewhat, I refer to the various rules and regulations and policies that restrict what can and cannot be done within a province simply as "**rules**" regardless of whether they are drawn from a statute, a regulation or some other source. I have opted to use the phrase "**diseases and disorders**" to refer collectively to all diseases, disorders, conditions and abnormal states that can affect the human body, regardless of the precise language used in the rules of a particular province. However, this is a form of shorthand and in all cases the statutes and regulations of your province should be consulted for the exact language used. Finally, when I refer to "**Restricted Activities**" I am referring to specific activities and procedures which, in certain provinces, may only be performed by members of Regulated Health Professions who are authorized to do so under that province's rules.

Contents

Chapter 1 Why Regulate? 9

Chapter 2 Overview of Regulation in Canada 13
    Regulating by Professional Exclusivity 14
    Regulating by Restricted Activities 15
    Use of Titles 17
    Prosecution of Holistic Nutritionists 18

Chapter 3 Provincial Rules & Regulations 25
    Alberta 29
    British Columbia 35
    Manitoba 41
    New Brunswick 48
    Newfoundland and Labrador 51
    Nova Scotia 53
    Ontario 58
    Prince Edward Island 62
    Quebec 65
    Saskatchewan 69

Chapter 4 Interpreting Key Terms 73
    Diagnosis 74
    Diseases & Disorders 75
    Drug 76
    Practice of Medicine 80
    Treatment 84

Chapter 5 Pulling It All Together 89
   Choose a Lawful Professional Title 89
   Avoid Using Medical Terms 90
   Avoid Diagnosing Diseases and Disorders 91
   Avoid Treating Diseases and Disorders if Practising Outside Alberta and Ontario. 93
   Know the Practice Restrictions That Apply Within Your Province 95
   Know Your Regulator 96
   Keep Current 97
   Practise Within the Scope of Your Training 97
   Use Appropriate Forms and Waivers 98
   Join a Good Professional Association 99
   Relax and Enjoy What You Do 100
Appendix 1 Assumption of Risk and Release of Liability For Nutrition Counselling Services 102

Chapter 1
Why Regulate?

It is often said within the Holistic Nutritionist community that the profession of a Holistic Nutritionist (and by this I mean an individual who provides nutritional consulting services to the public, but who is not a member of a Regulated Health Profession such as Medicine, or Dietetics, or Naturopathy) is not regulated in Canada. But this is an incorrect statement. While we in Canada pride ourselves in living in a free country, we all know that having freedom does not mean we are free to do whatever we please.

In the area of health services, rules have long existed to ensure those who purport to diagnose and treat illnesses have the requisite skill and knowledge to do so. The reasoning for this is very straightforward and understandable—the need to protect people, when they are at their weakest and most vulnerable (and very often most desperate), from the unscrupulous and incompetent who would prey upon them. This includes both those who sell remedies to the public and those who treat the sick.

Holistic Nutritionists, like everyone else in our society, are subject to these rules.

To understand why and how something as seemingly innocuous as the provision of nutrition advice is regulated, it is very important to keep in mind the consumer protection mandate. I say this because it is only by understanding the reason why a rule exists that we can fully understand how it is likely to be applied. So, before looking at the rules that apply to the practice of Holistic Nutrition, I believe it is worthwhile to briefly look at a few examples of medical shams and incompetent practice that give these rules purpose and meaning.

Webster's College Dictionary defines a *quack* to be "a fraudulent pretender of medical skill, a charlatan" and *Snake Oil* to be a "liquid concoction of questionable medical value sold as an all-purpose curative especially by travelling hucksters." To understand modern regulation, one must appreciate that our history is littered with such pretenders.

The period from the eighteenth century to the early twentieth century was a golden era for remedies commonly known as *patent medicines*. These elixirs were created at a time when very little was known about the biology of health and disease causation. As a result, patent medicines typically contained no (or virtually no) effective ingredients or nutritional content. In many cases the only active agents and the ingredients that tended to make a patient feel better were drugs such as morphine and alcohol. Patent medicines also tended to be promoted aggressively through wild miracle-like curative claims.

In 1889 and 1890, for example, while an influenza epidemic raged around the world, the Carbolic Smoke Ball Company sold its product, the Carbolic Smoke Ball, as a preventive and cure for the flu as well as several other diseases. The company even offered a £100 reward to anyone who contracted the flu while using its product. Unfortunately, the device did not contain any medicinal ingredients or nutritional supplements. Instead, it consisted of a rubber ball filled with carbolic acid, which was inhaled via a tube inserted into the nose. While the fumes would cause the user's nose to run, they did absolutely nothing to prevent or cure the flu or to reinforce the immune system. When a claim on the reward was finally made by Louisa Carlill, the company at first ignored her, and then tried to dodge its obligation to pay the reward by claiming she did not use their product correctly.[1]

Another outlandish case from the turn of the century involves a tonic known as "The Microbe Killer" and marketed under the telling image of a young man bashing a scythe from the hands of the skeleton of death with a baseball bat. This tonic was promoted as a curative for all diseases and claimed to work by killing the microbes that cause them. At its height, The Microbe Killer was manufactured in factories across the United States, and in England and Australia, for sale around the world. The tonic's creator, a gardener named William Radam, became very wealthy. Once again, however, the tonic did not cure all diseases—*any diseases*—or even provide a useful injection of vitamins for that matter. Upon analysis, its composition was shown to be more than 99% water with traces of sulphuric acid and red wine.

Equally important for consumer protection is the need to ensure practitioners have the education and skill required of their profession. An unskilled person with good intentions can do as much harm as a quack who is perfectly aware of the fraud he or she is perpetrating.

---

[1] For those who are interested in such things, Mrs. Carlill won her case. The decision, which is known as Carlill v. Carbolic Smoke Ball Company [1892] EWCA Civ 1, is a landmark decision in the advancement of contract law as it relates to unilateral contracts and still studied in law schools today.

The case of R v. Kish[2] involves the activities of Robert and Margo Kish, two *phytologists* (a system of healing that combines spiritualism and nutrition) charged with unlawfully practising Medicine. The charges against the Kishes arose from their attempt to cure their patient, Edward Pollack, of his terminal lung cancer using hydrogen peroxide (applied both internally and externally) and nutritional supplements. Such was their confidence they even purportedly counselled Mr. Pollack against taking chemotherapy and radiation treatments. Now, whatever your beliefs are about nutritional therapy, or about the use of hydrogen peroxide to fight cancer (and the Court was convinced of the sincerity of the Kishes' beliefs), I think we can all agree that nutritional counsellors are overstepping their training when they emphatically claim to have a cure for terminal stage lung cancer and counsel a client to suspend all conventional medical treatments. Mr. Pollack, of course, died within the time frame estimated by his doctor. The Kish's were found guilty of practising Medicine without a licence because they intentionally administered a treatment (hydrogen peroxide) for a disease (lung cancer).

These short stories illustrate the problem. As a Holistic Nutritionist you may have common sense, be honest, know the proper scope of your practice, only recommend foods and supplements with known and documented health benefits, and believe the rules are an unnecessary restriction on your freedom to help your clients. But if you are such a person, the rules do not really exist to protect the public from you. The rules exist to protect the public from the insincere and dishonest, and the people who lack proper training and common sense and who also live among us. You are just caught in the cross fire.

This said, it must also be recognized that sometimes the rules that regulate what we do serve other purposes as well. Sometimes they also end up protecting the old guard, creating monopolies and stifling innovation. This can be a big problem. While googling around on this subject[3], I came across several lists of some famous (and in some circles still infamous) scientists once labelled as quacks by their peers. Included among these were Thomas Allinson, the founder of naturopathy (a Regulated Health Profession in British Columbia, Manitoba, Ontario, Saskatchewan, Alberta and Nova Scotia); Samuel Hahnemann, the founder of homeopathy (homeopathic remedies are sold throughout Canada and regulated under the Natural Health Products Regulations under Canada's *Food and Drugs Act*); D.D. Palmer, the founder of Chiropractory (a Regulated Health Profession in all Canadian provinces); Ignac Semmelweis, a Hungarian physician who first advocated the importance of hand disinfection when treating patients; Louis Pasteur, who among other things, confirmed the germ theory of disease; and Linus Pauling, a Nobel Prize winner in chemistry who was widely ridiculed for

---

[2] R. v. Kish (1993), 12 Alta. L.R. (3d) 185
[3] Special thanks to the contributors to "Quackery," *Wikipedia: The Free Encyclopedia* [online]. Wikimedia Foundation, Inc. [Accessed February 17, 2011.] <http://en.wikipedia.org/wiki/Quackery>.

advocating the use of large doses of vitamin C to fight the common cold and the father of orthomolecular medicine.

There can be little doubt that many of these innovators faced regulatory restrictions that frustrated their ability to make advances in healthcare available to the public. Many Holistic Nutritionists also face this challenge. In most provinces a Holistic Nutritionist is prohibited from making a diagnosis and treating diseases and disorders. In some provinces they are even restricted from structuring diets to promote the health of their clients. Where this is the case it can be argued that such restrictions exist more to protect existing professional monopolies of one or more Regulated Health Professions than to protect the public. However, in reviewing the rules that apply to Holistic Nutritionists, this legitimate criticism of the system must be tempered by an understanding of the consumer protection mandate, because notwithstanding differences in philosophical approach, this is a primary objective of the regulators.

Chapter 2
Overview of Regulation in Canada

Canada is a federation of provinces and territories. This means the rules that govern our lives are promulgated by the federal and various provincial governments within each of their areas of jurisdiction and by our cities and municipalities within the jurisdictions that have been delegated to them. As a result, the regulation of health services in Canada is in many ways a patchwork quilt, with significant differences existing among our various provinces and regions.

The provision of health services to the public is primarily regulated by provincial governments. This means the task of describing what a Holistic Nutritionist can and cannot do in Canada must be done on a province-by-province basis. What may be lawful in Alberta, for example, may result in a fine or even imprisonment if practiced in Nova Scotia. In the next chapter, the reader will find legislative summaries for each of the provinces setting out the rules that impact on the ability of a Holistic Nutritionist (remember, the unregulated kind) to provide nutritional advice to clients.

Within Canada, there are essentially two approaches used to regulate the provision of health services: (1) professional exclusivity—where the rules prohibit anyone other than members of a profession from carrying on the business and practice of that profession (e.g., only members of the provincial College of Physicians may practice Medicine); and (2) restricted activities—where the rules create a list of defined activities and procedures that may only be performed by members of Regulated Health Professions that have been granted the authority to do so (e.g., only members of the provincial College of Physicians may reset or cast a bone fracture).

Regulating by Professional Exclusivity

The first approach, regulation by professional exclusivity, is the traditional approach used for regulating health services. Historically, this approach began with the recognition of the medical profession as a discrete profession and the delegation to it of the right and obligation to regulate its own standards and members, the theory essentially being that Medicine is a highly specialized activity and members of the profession are in a better position than the public to know the qualifications and standards that should apply to practitioners.[4]

Over the years the concept of what constituted the practice of Medicine fragmented as new health practices emerged and specialties within the traditional field of Medicine developed and splintered off. Eventually, many of these new health professions sought the prestige and benefits of professional status and petitioned governments for the right of self-governance. Today, somewhere between twenty and thirty health professions are recognized and granted the right of self-regulation within most provinces.

While this approach to regulation appears simple, it actually can lead to confusion because these statutes often do not properly define the activities that constitute the practice of the profession they regulate, instead leaving this task to the governing body of the profession itself and the courts.

Using the practice of Medicine as an example, common sense should tell us that performing surgery, setting broken bones, diagnosing a disease such as cancer and prescribing and administering chemotherapy as a treatment involves the practice of Medicine. But what about less obvious activities? What about determining whether a person is obese and structuring a healthy diet for him or her? Diagnosing obesity is relatively easy. It can be done with little more evidence than our eyes, and the treatment for it (exercise and diet) is also pretty straightforward. Yet, obesity is also a recognized disease. Does the act of identifying and treating obesity constitute the practice of Medicine? To take this argument to its extreme, what about dehydration and starvation? If I tell a dehydrated person to drink water or a starving person to eat food, am I diagnosing and treating a condition? What if I recommend they take vitamins?

For Holistic Nutritionists who want to ensure they do not cross the line and face a charge of unlawfully practising Medicine this gray zone is a real problem.

---

[4] Casey, J. T., *The Regulation of Professions in Canada* (Toronto: Carswell, 1988).

In Canada, the provinces of Manitoba[5], New Brunswick, Newfoundland and Labrador, Nova Scotia, Prince Edward Island and Saskatchewan currently regulate the provision of health services using this approach and B.C., which is in the midst of changing how it regulates health services, is operating a hybrid model. Holistic Nutritionists operating within these provinces must comply with all rules contained in all of the various statutes and regulations that create the Regulated Health Professions within their province of residence.

Most schools that educate and train Holistic Nutritionists teach that the practice of Holistic Nutrition involves the assessment and promotion of health and wellness. When faced with clients in ill health, however, it can be very tempting to move beyond this and to start diagnosing and/or treating suspected and known conditions. As a result, it is particularly important for Holistic Nutritionists to understand the boundaries of Regulated Health Professions whose professional practices include the diagnosis of diseases and disorders and the use of nutrition and supplements both as treatments and to promote health. Of particular concern, therefore, are the statutes and regulations that define the professional practice of Medicine, which is both regulated and restricted in all provinces, Dietetics, which is regulated in all provinces, but only restricted in some, and Naturopathy, which is regulated and restricted only in some provinces.

In the next chapter, I have included summaries of key provisions from these statutes, organized on a province-by-province basis, for easy reference.

Regulating by Restricted Activities

The other regulatory approach taken by Canadian provinces involves focusing more directly on consumer protection by controlling who may perform specific defined acts and procedures (which I will refer to as Restricted Activities throughout this book) that are viewed as involving risk and therefore requiring a minimum level of skill and training. For example, section 4(1) of Schedule 7.1 to the Alberta *Government Organization Act* provides in part:

> **4(1)** No person shall perform a restricted activity or a portion of it on or for another person unless:
>
> (a) the person performing it
>
> (i) is a regulated member as defined in the Health Professions Act, and is authorized to perform it by the regulations under the *Health Professions Act* . . .

---

[5] Manitoba is currently in the process of changing how it regulates Health Professions. An overview of the changes it is implementing can be found in Chapter 3.

The list of Restricted Activities is defined in section 2(1) of the same schedule and provides in part:

> **2(1)** The following, carried out in relation to or as part of providing a health service, are restricted activities:
>> (a) to cut a body tissue, to administer anything by an invasive procedure on body tissue or to perform surgical or other invasive procedures on body tissue
>>> (i) below the dermis or the mucous membrane or in or below the surface of the cornea;
>>>
>>> (ii) in or below the surface of teeth, including scaling of teeth; . . .

Regulation through Restricted Activities represents the emerging trend among Canadian provinces. At the present time, the provinces of Ontario, Alberta and Quebec have implemented Restricted Activity regulatory regimes and the provinces of B.C. and Manitoba are in the midst of making the transition to one. This approach is now being favoured because it addresses the reality that many health professions have practice areas that both overlap and include procedures that can be safely and economically performed by unregulated professionals. In a consultation document prepared by the Government of Manitoba, the effect and benefit of moving to a "Reserved Act" (i.e., Restricted Activity) approach was described as follows:

> Actions or clinical procedures that may present a demonstrable risk of harm to the public will be regulated. Many of the reserved acts can be performed by more than one profession, so collaborative care will be encouraged. These acts and procedures will be restricted to specified practitioners, so unregulated practitioners will only be able to provide them if authorized under the legislation, e.g., under delegation from a regulated health profession. Unregulated practitioners will be able to provide services that do not include reserved acts. This model will help improve patient safety.[6]

This trend is good news for Holistic Nutritionists. The move toward identifying and reserving only higher risk activities for the exclusive domain of specific Regulated Health Professions generally[7] means there is more room for practice than in provinces where regulation occurs through professional exclusivity. And because these activities are defined in the rules, there is also less doubt about what Holistic Nutritionists can and cannot do.

---

[6] Health Professions Regulatory Reform Consultation Document, Proposed Umbrella Health Professions Legislation: the *Regulated Health Professions Act,* Government of Manitoba, January 2009.

[7] The province of Quebec, which aggressively enforces its prohibition against 'prescribing treatment' is a notable exception to this rule.

This said, the world for Holistic Nutritionists in the Restricted Activities provinces is still not perfect. Many will find the rules against diagnosing and treating diseases and disorders, which exist to varying degrees in the different provinces, both unnecessary and too broadly defined. Borrowing from an earlier example, is one "treating" an illness by telling a client to take vitamins to remedy a deficiency? As well, there are some fairly significant differences among the provinces about what procedures are restricted. In Alberta, for example, neither the diagnosis nor treatment of a disease or disorder is a Restricted Activity. In Ontario, the diagnosis of a disease in circumstances "in which it is reasonably foreseeable that the individual or his or her personal representative will rely on the diagnosis" is restricted, but the treatment of a previously diagnosed diseases or disorder is not. In Quebec, both the diagnosis and treatment of a disease and disorders are Restricted Activities and aggressively enforced.

In the next chapter, I have included summaries of key provisions of these rules, organized on a province-by-province basis, for easy reference.

Use of Titles

As part of regulating health professions and/or activities that are restricted and may only be performed by specified Regulated Health Professions, the provinces also restrict the use of professional titles, essentially reserving the use of titles typically associated with a profession, for the exclusive use of its members. The principle behind this is, obviously, consumer protection. If the primary purpose of regulating a profession is to ensure the quality of practitioners, it makes sense to ensure those practitioners can be readily identified by the public. An exclusive title does this.

In Canada, most provinces generally reserve titles such as "Doctor" and "Physician" and "Surgeon" and associated abbreviations for use by a member of one or more of the "medical" professions (e.g., Medicine, Dentistry, Psychiatry, etc.). In Alberta this restrictive list extends to approximately 75 specific "specialties of Medicine." In provinces in which Naturopathy is a Regulated Health Profession, use of titles such as "Naturopath" and "Naturopathic Doctor" are similarly restricted.

The use of the title "Dietitian" is generally reserved for use by registered Dietitians in all provinces. In three provinces, Alberta, Nova Scotia and Quebec, the title "Nutritionist" or "Registered Nutritionist" is also reserved. In addition, several provinces restrict the use of any other title or claim that may wrongly indicate a person is a member of a provincially Regulated Health Profession.

Where a title is reserved for use by one or more Regulated Health Professions, it is unlawful for a person who is not a member of one of those professions to use the title. Since there are wide differences among the provinces about which titles are reserved for use by the various Regulated Health Professions, it is very important to check the rules that exist in one's province.

In the next chapter, I have included summaries of the key rules, organized on a province-by-province basis, for easy reference.

Prosecution of Holistic Nutritionists

In working with Holistic Nutritionists over the years, I have noticed the existence of a popular belief that Holistic Nutritionists are frequently prosecuted (I should almost say persecuted) for doing little more than providing sound nutritional advice to their clients. If this were the case, there should be a significant body of case law (i.e., reported Court decisions) that can be used to define the appropriate scope of practice and the point(s) at which a nutritionist's actions may cross the line into the areas of Medicine, Naturopathy, or Dietetics.

To my surprise, I could not locate a single reported case in Canada of a Holistic Nutritionist being charged with unlawful practice of Medicine, Naturopathy or Dietetics. I located only two hybrid cases involving nutritional counselling in conjunction with other activities and one case involving a Homeopath providing services that, in part, are sometimes provided by Holistic Nutritionists.

Concerned that my research was somehow missing the mark, I contacted several of the provincial regulatory colleges, including the Colleges of Physicians and Surgeons of Ontario, British Columbia, Quebec and Saskatchewan, to obtain their perspective on the prosecution of Holistic Nutritionists.

A representative of the College of Physicians and Surgeons of Ontario told me their jurisdiction extended only over its members, and that they forwarded any complaints (which they rarely received) about non-members to the local police. From there, I followed up with both the Ontario Provincial Police and Toronto Police. The Toronto Police were unable (or unwilling) to refer me to a desk within their organization that would handle such a complaint. A detective with the Ontario Provincial Police confirmed his desk would deal with this issue, but he told me he could not remember a single incident of investigating and charging a Holistic Nutritionist. When asked what I should take from this, I was informed that it didn't mean it didn't happen, as he could not speak for the entire force, but that, obviously, such incidences were extremely rare. Why? The officer surmised that individuals who seek out alternative health practitioners tended not to complain when those services did not comply with medical standards, and that without a complaint there is nothing to investigate.

This perspective was echoed by a representative of the Colleges of Physicians and Surgeons of Saskatchewan who informed me the College had formally adopted a policy of respecting the right of consumers to choose their own health services modality, in part, as a result of the difficulty of proceeding against alternative health service providers where clients refused to cooperate. I was told the College now focuses its efforts on cases of fraud (e.g., impersonation of a doctor) and where the service provider causes injury to the patient.

By contrast, the representative of the Quebec College of Physicians and Surgeons with whom I spoke said the Quebec College is very active in protecting consumers and prosecuting individuals for wrongful practice of Medicine. But their concern was with anyone who was not a member of a Regulated Health Profession, which includes Holistic Nutritionists in Quebec but also Naturopaths and others. I was referred to a brief[8] prepared by the College of Physicians of Quebec in 1993 that is still referred to as embodying the College's view on alternative therapies:

> Most Quebec physicians, without fanfare and without masquerading under the "holistic" title have for a long time treated their patient as a whole person (global approach). Many "alternative therapies" parade under the holistic concept banner. . . . "Alternative therapies" for the most part, have not been proven scientifically or claim to be untestable by the usual scientific methods.

While this perspective may not be good news for Holistic Nutritionists in Quebec, it does mean at least that they are not being singled out.

So what do the results of my legal research and informal enquiries mean?

First, I suspect the paucity of reported cases indicates Holistic Nutritionists are not being singled out and prosecuted (or persecuted) for unlawful practice of Medicine. Second, I suspect it indicates that most Holistic Nutritionists are practising within the laws of their province and are not generally engaged in diagnosing or treating diseases or misusing professional titles. Third, I suspect it indicates enforcement is often practiced informally through the use of warnings, at least in instances where no one has been harmed by the Holistic Nutritionist's actions. Finally, and most importantly, I suspect it means most Holistic

---

[8] Brief on Alternative Therapies, 1993. Submitted by the College of Physicians of Quebec to the Commission of Social Affairs.

Nutritionists are providing safe, useful advice to clients who are seeking an alternative path to wellness than that offered by traditional Medicine.

So turning now to the cases I did find, what can they tell us?

The first of these cases is R v. Kish, the facts of which I briefly summarized in Chapter 1. This case involved two phytologists, Robert and Margo Kish, who were charged with the unlawful practice of Medicine contrary to s. 76(1)(a) of the Alberta *Medical Profession Act*[9] for prescribing hydrogen peroxide and nutritional supplements to treat the terminal lung cancer of their deceased client, Mr. Ed Pollack.

The Court's decision turned on section 77(1) of the Act, which defined the practice of Medicine to include the prescription or administration of any treatment "for the prevention, alleviation or cure of any human disease, ailment, deformity, defect or injury." So the key question for the Court was whether their activities constituted a "treatment" of a "human disease, ailment, deformity, defect or injury." The brother of the deceased (who had attended at the home of the Kishes with the deceased) testified that the Kishes ridiculed the medical profession, counselled against radiation and chemotherapy, and assured the deceased that they could cure his cancer.

For their part, the Kishes testified that as phytologists they devised programs for their clients that were a combination of spiritual, mental and nutritional benefits. They also argued that they had not been told of the extent of Ed Pollack's cancer. The judge summarized their testimony as follows:

> Robert Kish stated that their approach was to look at the whole body and to try and devise a program to deal with the needs of the whole person. He did go so far as to admit that "where there is a weakness within the system we try to regenerate that". With respect to the hydrogen peroxide therapy he indicated that the theory was that it was an "oxygenator" and it would also give a boost of energy and that they recommend a regime of vitamins and minerals with the hydrogen peroxide program to deal with what they thought was a small cancerous spot on his lung.

From this passage, it appears the Kishes were arguing they did not treat diseases per se but rather the whole person, with the goal of moving their clients toward wellness, which seems fairly close to the goals of a Holistic Nutritionist and an argument a Holistic Nutritionist might make about his or her own practice.

---

[9] This statute is no longer in force, having been replaced by *The Health Professions Act*.

The Court found the Kishes guilty of unlawfully practising Medicine. Interestingly, it was not the prescription of vitamins and minerals or even an intravenous injection of B12 they gave Mr. Pollack that proved to be the problem. The court did not appear to be concerned with their efforts to boost Mr. Pollack's overall health and did not even evaluate whether such activities constituted a treatment. Instead, the smoking gun was the prescription of the hydrogen peroxide and their claim that it was a cure.

> On the basis of all of the evidence there is no doubt in my mind that what the Kishes did was prescribe a course of treatment clearly directed at and purporting to be able to cure the cancer that Pollack suffered from. By whatever definition of "treatment" is used (and I would refer specifically to those definitions used by Cooke J. in *R. v. Ringrose* (1989), 94 A.R. 350 (Q.B.), at p. 353) the prescribing of hydrogen peroxide to be taken internally for the purpose of killing cancer cells and curing cancer falls squarely within even the narrowest interpretation of "treatment."

The other quasi-nutritionist case I was able to uncover was R. v. Windrum,[10] a decision of the Saskatchewan Court of Queen's Bench, involving the appeal of Mr. Windrum from a charge of unlawfully practising Medicine contrary to the Saskatchewan *Medical Profession Act*.

The facts of this case are in many ways (with one major exception) similar to the experiences, I believe, many Holistic Nutritionists have every day. The accused did not claim or pretend to be a doctor. The client (or more accurately the mother of the client, since the actual patient was an infant girl) was also aware that the treatments recommended by Mr. Windrum were typically different than those prescribed by doctors. Mr. Windrum examined the infant physically, enquired into her medical history, drew blood from the infant girl's finger and examined it under a microscope. He diagnosed the girl as suffering from "parasites, liver impairment, liver damage, liver stress, yeast problems, deficient bone marrow, overactive spleen, inflamed spleen, genetically weak bladder, pre-cancerous condition, lymph congestion, and genetic heart condition" largely on the basis of his analysis of the blood sample.

Mr. Windrum was charged with breaching the Saskatchewan *Medical Profession Act* for diagnosing each of these conditions and for treating the infant girl by prescribing iron supplements, vitamins and other substances. Under the *Medical Profession Act* both diagnosing and treating a disease or disorder were deemed to be the practice of Medicine.

For Holistic Nutritionists there are two aspects of this case that, I believe, are of particular interest.

---

[10] R. v. Windrum, [1995] 2 W.W.R. 226

First, Mr. Windrum tried to argue that as he did not hold himself out to be a doctor and did not claim to practice Medicine, he could not be found to have practiced Medicine. The Court ruled his intentions to be irrelevant:

> Windrum argued that his acts were either not intended or not perceived as practising medicine. In my view that is not relevant. The issue before the Court is whether he was practising medicine. In other words, was he diagnosing or treating patients.

Second, in deciding whether Mr. Windrum diagnosed and/or treated a disease, the Court turned to a medical doctor as an expert witness and accepted the doctor's assessment that both Mr. Windrum's diagnosis and treatment conformed to procedures that could be followed within Medicine:

> Dr. Loewen, who was qualified as an expert, said that the diagnosis is a conclusion about the patient's condition based on her history, physical examination and tests if necessary. He went on to state that one can diagnose by examining the patient's blood. Furthermore, many of the conditions found by Windrum could be diagnosed by following the above process. In Dr. Loewen's opinion it was common practice to treat patients by prescribing vitamins or iron supplements.

It is not surprising that Mr. Windrum was found to have provided a diagnosis. He clearly examined his patient, including through a blood test, and provided a detailed list of conditions and ailments detected. And perhaps it is not surprising that the Court found the simple prescription of vitamins and supplements to constitute administering a treatment, as they were prescribed in response to the conditions diagnosed. But it is also clear in this case that the Court did not like or respect Mr. Windrum, and it is possible that this impacted on the Court's willingness to find the prescription of vitamins to be administering a treatment. In commenting on the reasonableness of the sentence ($5,000 in fines) the Court noted:

> In this case Windrum's actions were improper and unethical. After obtaining the trust of Loni and her mother he then attempted, without any training or expertise, to diagnose Loni. After frightening both Loni and her mother by claiming that the child suffered from many serious medical conditions, he then sought to profit from his actions.

> Windrum is a danger to the public and therefore any sentence imposed must reflect both general and individual deterrence. In my view the sentences imposed are entirely appropriate and therefore the sentence appeal is also dismissed.

The final case I discovered that is of interest is R. v. Sandhar,[11] an appeal decision of the Alberta Court of Queen's Bench, overturning the acquittal at trial of Mr. Sandhar for practising Homeopathy. Mr. Sandhar was charged with breaching sections 76 and 77 of the Alberta *Medical Profession Act*, which as we saw in the Kish case, prohibited the practice of Medicine without a licence, and deemed the practice of Medicine to include claiming the ability to diagnose and/or treat human disease and illness, and administering treatment.

What is of particular interest for Holistic Nutritionists is that the diagnostic procedures and treatment prescribed by Mr. Sandhar were not the kind that would be prescribed by a typical medical physician. In fact, his diagnostic process—which centred on body energy levels—is similar to the practice of muscle testing used by many Holistic Nutritionists, and his treatments—an herbal supplement and a liver cleanser—are of the type recommended by many Holistic Nutritionists daily.

The facts are clearly set out in this extract from the decision:

> On April 23, 1985, Peggy Lewis attended the Respondent's clinic in Edmonton and told him that she had a feeling of tiredness and sluggishness, occasional backache and shortness of breath. Following Dr. LeRiche's instructions, she indicated that her doctor was thinking of examining her for thyroid problems. The Respondent had Miss Lewis fill out a questionnaire and inquired about her lifestyle and diet. He then carried out what he called an "Alert Test". The machine that was used had one rod connected to it which was placed in one of Miss Lewis' hands. This rod was moistened with a compound. Another rod was connected to a machine and the Respondent conducted an examination of Miss Lewis by touching various spots on her fingernails and toes.
>
> The Respondent testified that the readings from the machine indicated that Miss Lewis had possible lung congestion. The circulation reading was low which accounted for Miss Lewis having cold extremities. His testing also indicated that there was an inflammation of the liver and kidneys. It was the Respondent's belief that there was a build up of toxins which would be the cause of her tiredness and sluggishness.
>
> The Respondent had Miss Lewis purchase from him two bottles of drugs, one which was said to be a liver cleanser which would help her liver problems and the other was Camphora which was to alleviate the feelings of tiredness.
>
> Miss Lewis was charged $30.00 for a consultation fee, $10.00 for the liver cleanser and $5.00 for the Camphora.

---

[11] R v. Sandhar (1988), 86 A.R. 241

Concerning the mysterious machine used to diagnose Ms. Lewis:

> The Alert Test machine that was used by the Respondent was said by the Respondent to be used to determine a person's state of health as a precautionary measure but has nothing to do with homoeopathy. The Respondent stated the machine is designed to measure the flow of energy of various organs from acqua pressure meridian points and is a test technique he was trained in by the Society of Ultramolecular Medicine in Las Vegas.

Mr. Sandhar was ultimately found to have practised Medicine in breach of the Alberta *Medical Act*. In reaching this decision, it did not matter to the Court that Mr. Sandhar was following a discipline that was different from conventional western Medicine, because the Act deemed even the making of a claim to diagnose illness and the act of prescribing a treatment to be within the scope of the practice of Medicine.

Chapter 3
Provincial Rules & Regulations

The purpose of this chapter is to review the rules that restrict the right of Holistic Nutritionists to carry on a conventional practice, which for my purposes I define to mean assessing the health of paying clients and recommending dietary changes, foods and nutritional supplements to improve health or address known diseases and conditions.

As mentioned in the last chapter, since this book is intended for use by individuals who are not members of a provincially regulated health profession, this goal must be achieved by way of subtraction. Meaning, since there are no rules stipulating what Holistic Nutritionists may do, we must instead look at what they are prohibited from doing. While this may seem a simple way of proceeding, it does carry with it a serious procedural difficulty. In Canada there are literally thousands of statutes regulating what we can and cannot do, and investigating, assessing and summarizing all of these would fill volumes.

Out of necessity I have, therefore, established a few ground rules to narrow the scope of my enquiry and to keep my discussion on point. In relying upon this book, the reader must keep in mind that it is not an exhaustive study of all rules that impact upon a Holistic Nutritionist's practice. Rather, it is a summary of the laws that restrict or prohibit the activities of a normal practice, along the lines of my definition at the start of this chapter.

So what are these ground rules?

First, I have restricted my focus to reviewing rules that exist in respect to the three Regulated Health Professions that most overlap with the practice of Holistic Nutritionists: Medicine, Dietetics and Naturopathy. The reason for looking at the practices of Medicine and Naturopathy is obvious. Both of these professions involve assessing health, diagnosing illness and disease and prescribing treatments that may include nutrition. Historically, Medicine can also be thought of as the "root" health profession. By this I mean, the imposition of rules on what the unlicensed world can and cannot do with respect to diagnosing and treating human diseases and conditions began with Medicine, and it remains the largest and most broadly defined professional practice area in health.

I have included Dietetics for the obvious reason that this profession is the "Regulated Health Profession" in all provinces for nutritional advisors.[12]

As the reader may appreciate, this means I have not looked at and will not be discussing many, many other health professions such as Psychotherapy, Massage Therapy, Chiropractics, and Chinese Medicine, all of which are regulated in one or more and in most cases all provinces. And the various provincial statutes that regulate them (at least in the provinces that do not regulate using the "Restricted Activities" approach discussed in the last chapter) may restrict persons who are not licensed from practising these professions. However, it is also my assumption that these professions are sufficiently dissimilar from the practice of Holistic Nutrition that a well-intentioned and formally educated Holistic Nutritionist is not likely to accidently lapse into their practice. If, however, your practice does include advice and procedures that go beyond assessing wellness and providing nutritional advice, you should investigate the rules that apply to these and other Regulated Health Professions in your province.

Second, I have limited my scope to statutes that relate to whether a Holistic Nutritionist can carry on a conventional practice. Accordingly, I have not reviewed or summarized the many statutes of general application that might regulate how (rather than whether) these services are provided.

For example, many provinces maintain statutes that specifically regulate the collection, storage, use, release and disposal of personal information and client records. In Ontario, for example, the applicable statute is the *Personal Health Information Protection Act*, and it does apply to both regulated and unregulated health professionals. And all Canadians must comply with the federal government's *Personal Information Protection and Electronic Documents*

---

[12] On its web site, http://collegeofdietitiansofbc.org/about-dietitians (accessed January 15, 2011), The College of Dietitians of British Columbia describes the practice of a Dietitian as follows: "...assessing nutritional needs of individuals and groups; designing implementing and monitoring nutritional care plans and therapeutic diets based on current and relevant scientific, medical and nutrition information; disseminating relevant scientific information about food and human nutrition to promote health and assist individuals, groups and communities attain and maintain health; and managing quality food service operations in healthcare institutions."

Act (PIPEDA), which establishes rules for the collection, use and disclosure of personal information by private organizations in the course of commercial activities. Provinces also have statutes regulating the dispensing of drugs, the preparation, storage and sale of foods, and a host of other matters that may be of interest to a Holistic Practitioner depending upon the scope of his or her business.

To further complicate the regulatory landscape, it must also be remembered that regions and municipalities have the authority to regulate businesses that operate within their borders and may require someone who wants to carry on an otherwise lawful business to obtain a licence. In the city of Toronto, for example, the Municipal Code requires anyone who provides "Holistic Services" (which is defined to include any modality used as a tool for therapeutic and wellness purposes other than body rubs and services provided by members of Regulated Health Professions) and any location at which Holistic Services are provided, to be licensed.

These rules and many others must also be complied with, and I recommend that a lawyer who is licensed to practice in your province be consulted before opening your practice so you are aware of them.

Finally, I have not investigated or summarized laws of general application such as the Criminal Code, (which may be a factor, if one is charged with fraud) but which apply to all of us equally, regardless of whether we carry on a health services business.

By omitting all of these areas of enquiry, I am not claiming they are not relevant and have no bearing on the operation of an unregistered, unlicensed nutritional health practice. Such statutes are very relevant and must be complied with and one should always consult a lawyer to ensure one does comply. However, the review of all of their implications across ten different provinces of Canada is simply a task that is beyond the scope of this book.

Now a few comments about what is included in this chapter.

In the pages that follow I have set out extracts from the key statutes and regulations that restrict the provision of health services organized on a province-by-province basis, for easy reference. To review the rules for a particular province, simply turn to the summary for that province.

As previously mentioned, some provinces regulate the provision of health services by establishing a list of Restricted Activities. Where this is the case, these activities may not be performed except (1) by a member of a Regulated Health Profession whose members are expressly authorized to do so (typically, members of the medical profession are authorized to perform all or nearly all Restricted Activities, while members of other Regulated Health

Professions are authorized to perform a subset of activities, or none at all), or (2) the situation falls within one of the limited exceptions set out in the rules. These exceptions differ from province to province but generally include providing the service under the immediate supervision of a person who is authorized to perform the activity in question, as part of spiritual counselling, or as emergency first aid. As these exceptions do not create an exception for provision of nutritional advice, I have not included them in my summaries.

In reviewing the rules, the reader will come across terms and phrases such as "practice of Medicine" and "diagnose" and "treatment" that are either not or only superficially defined. In Chapter 4, I review how the Courts and other legal authorities have defined some of these terms, to provide greater insight into their meaning.

I have included in the legislative summaries information concerning the use of professional titles. For expediency, I have not summarized the professional titles reserved for Medical practitioners and Naturopaths, as these titles (Physician, Doctor, MD, Naturopath, etc.) are not descriptive of or typically associated with the provision of nutritional health advice, and therefore, are not likely to be used accidentally by a well-intentioned Holistic Nutritionist. So my review centres on titles reserved for use by registered Dietitians.

Finally, it must always be remembered that the rules I have cited in this book are subject to change at any time and therefore cannot be relied upon to be complete, accurate or even in force at the time of reading. For certainty, the reader should always consult a lawyer or the actual statutes and regulations in place within his or her province at the time the information is required.

Alberta

Provision of health services in Alberta is regulated primarily through the *Health Professions Act* and Schedule 7.1 to the *Government Organization Act*.

The *Health Professions Act* establishes the various Regulated Health Professions and the rules that apply to their operation as self-governing professions. Schedule 7.1 to the *Government Organization Act* establishes the Restricted Activities that may be performed only by members of a Regulated Health Profession who are authorized to perform one or more of the Restricted Activities. A person who is not a member of a Regulated Health Profession may not perform any of these procedures.

In Alberta one is required to register under the *Health Professions Act*, (i.e., be a member of a Regulated Health Profession) if he or she meets the education, experience and other qualifications for a Regulated Health Profession **and** intends to provide, among other things, a service that comes within the scope of practice of a Regulated Health Profession to the public or "food and nutrition professional services that are used by other regulated members and individuals to provide services directly to the public." So, for example, if someone meets the requirements of The College of Dietitians of Alberta to be a Registered Dietitian and Nutritionist and wishes to provide the services to the public of a Dietitian and Nutritionist[13], that person must become a member of the college. Failing to do so constitutes a breach of the Act and may result in a fine of $2,000 for a first offence.

Schedule 23 of the *Health Professions Act* reserves the title "Registered Nutritionist" (among others) for use by members of The College of Dietitians. Because the rules do not restrict the use of the word "Nutritionist" on its own, the use of the word "Nutritionist" either on its own or in combination with any word other than "Registered" (for example "Holistic Nutritionist") is, strictly speaking, permitted. However, because the *Health Professions Act* also contains

---

[13] Schedule 23 "Profession of Registered Dietitians and Registered Nutritionists" to the *Health Professions Act* allows registered dietitians and registered nutritionists to do one or more of the following:
(a) assess nutritional status and develop, implement and evaluate food and nutrition strategies and interventions to promote health and treat illness,
(b) apply food and nutrition principles to the management of food service systems and to the development and analysis of food and food products,
(c) promote optimal health, food security and food safety through the development and delivery of food and nutrition education, programs and policies,
(c.1) teach, manage and conduct research in the science, techniques and practice of dietetics, and
(d) provide restricted activities authorized by the regulations.

some fairly broad rules against using a title that wrongly implies one is a member of a Regulated Health Profession, it should only be used as part of a longer title that is substantially different from "Registered Nutritionist."

A Holistic Nutritionist who is not a member of a Regulated Health Profession in Alberta may carry on a conventional nutritional practice provided he or she: (1) is not required to become a member of the College of Dietitians of Alberta by virtue of meeting the requirements of the College for registration: (2) does not perform a Restricted Activity described in Schedule 7.1 of the *Government Organization Act*; (3) does not market themselves to the public using a title reserved for Registered Dietitians and Nutritionists, Medical Doctors, Naturopaths or any another Regulated Health Profession; and (4) otherwise complies with laws of general application.

I have set out, on the following pages, the list of Restricted Activities from Schedule 7 of *Alberta's Government Organization Act* in its entirety. Interestingly, the activities of diagnosing and treating diseases and disorders are not restricted. So Holistic Nutritionists in Alberta are permitted to diagnose and treat diseases and disorders provided they do not perform a Restricted Activity (e.g., prescribing drugs). Recommending dietary changes, over the counter food supplements and natural health products are not restricted.

Restrictions on Activities in Alberta

Government Organization Act
c. G-10 Schedule 7.1

s. 2(1) The following, carried out in relation to or as part of providing a health service, are restricted activities:

    (a)   to cut a body tissue, to administer anything by an invasive procedure on body tissue or to perform surgical or other invasive procedures on body tissue

        (i)   below the dermis or the mucous membrane or in or below the surface of the cornea;

        (ii)   in or below the surface of teeth, including scaling of teeth;

    (b)   to insert or remove instruments, devices, fingers or hands

        (i)   beyond the cartilaginous portion of the ear canal,

        (ii)   beyond the point in the nasal passages where they normally narrow,

        (iii)   beyond the pharynx,

        (iv)   beyond the opening of the urethra,

        (v)   beyond the labia majora,

(vi) beyond the anal verge, or

(vii) into an artificial opening into the body;

(b.1) to insert into the ear canal

(i) under pressure, liquid, air or gas;

(ii) a substance that subsequently solidifies;

(c) to set or reset a fracture of a bone;

(d) to reduce a dislocation of a joint except for a partial dislocation of the joints of the fingers and toes;

(e) to use a deliberate, brief, fast thrust to move the joints of the spine beyond the normal range but within the anatomical range of motion, which generally results in an audible click or pop;

(f) to prescribe a Schedule 1 drug within the meaning of the *Pharmacy and Drug Act*;[14]

(g) to dispense, compound, provide for selling or sell a Schedule 1 drug or Schedule 2 drug within the meaning of the *Pharmacy and Drug Act*;

(h) to administer a vaccine or parenteral nutrition;

(i) to prescribe, compound or administer blood or blood products;

(j) to prescribe or administer diagnostic imaging contrast agents;

(k) to prescribe or administer anesthetic gases, including nitrous oxide, for the purposes of anesthesia or sedation;

(l) to prescribe or administer radiopharmaceuticals, radiolabelled substances, radioactive gases or radioaerosols;

(m) to order or apply any form of ionizing radiation in

(i) medical radiography,

(ii) nuclear medicine, or

(iii) radiation therapy;

(n) to order or apply non-ionizing radiation in

(i) lithotripsy,

(ii) magnetic resonance imaging, or

(iii) ultrasound imaging, including any application of ultrasound to a fetus;

(o) to prescribe or fit

(i) an orthodontic or periodontal appliance,

(ii) a fixed or removable partial or complete denture, or

(iii) an implant supported prosthesis;

---

[14] Schedule 1 and Schedule 2 drugs do not include Natural Health Products as defined by the *Natural Health Products Regulations* to the *Canada Food and Drugs Act*.

(p) to perform a psychosocial intervention with an expectation of treating a substantial disorder of thought, mood, perception, orientation or memory that grossly impairs

    (i) judgment,

    (ii) behaviour,

    (iii) capacity to recognize reality, or

    (iv) ability to meet the ordinary demands of life;

(q) to manage labour or deliver a baby;

(r) to prescribe or dispense corrective lenses.

s. (2) Despite subsection (1), the following are not restricted activities:

(a) activities of daily living[15], whether performed by the individual or by a surrogate on the individual's behalf,

(b) giving information and providing advice with the intent of enhancing personal development, providing emotional support or promoting spiritual growth of individuals, couples, families and groups, and

(c) drawing venous blood.

Restrictions on Professional Titles in Alberta

Health Professions Act
c. H-7

s. 128(1) No person or group of persons shall represent or imply that the person is a regulated member or that the group of persons consists of regulated members unless the person is a regulated member or the group of persons consists of regulated members.

(2) No person or group of persons shall use the name of a college, alone or in combination with other words, in a manner that states or implies that the person or group of persons is a college under this Act unless the person or group of persons is a college under this Act.

(3) No regulated member shall use the word "registered" in a manner that states or implies that the member is a regulated member of a regulated profession except in accordance with the regulations.

---

[15] a) "activity of daily living" means an activity that individuals normally perform on their own behalf to maintain their health and well-being, and includes

 (i) routine and invasive self-care activities, including but not restricted to the removal of slivers and the cleaning of wounds, and

 (ii) specifically taught procedures, which generally result in predictable and stable responses, including but not restricted to catheterization, maintenance of drainage tubes and administration of drugs by injection;

(4) No person or group of persons shall use the word "regulated" in connection with the name of a regulated profession or professional service or the words "regulated health professional" in a manner that states or implies that the person or group of persons is a college or a regulated member or group of regulated members unless the person or group of persons is a college under this Act or another enactment or is a regulated member or consists of a group of regulated members.

(5) No person other than

    (a) a regulated member shall use a title, abbreviation or initials set out in section 2 of a schedule to this Act alone or in combination with other words in a manner that states or implies that the person is a regulated member of the college to which section 2 of the schedule refers, or

    (b) a student who is enrolled in a program that in the opinion of the registrar is a program to train persons to provide professional services shall use a title, abbreviation or initials set out in section 2 of a schedule to this Act in combination with the word "student" while undertaking activities related to the program.

(5.1) Despite subsections (1), (3), (5) and (10), a student described in subsection (5)(b) shall not use the title "regulated" or "registered" or the initial "R" in combination with the word "student" while undertaking activities related to a program described in subsection (5)(b).

(6) No corporation shall use the word college, alone or in combination with other words, in a manner that states or implies that the corporation is a college under this Act unless the corporation is a college under this Act or authorized to use the word college under another enactment.

(7) No person shall use the title "doctor", "surgeon", "pathologist" or "oncologist" or the abbreviation "Dr." alone or in combination with other words in connection with providing a health service unless the person is authorized to use the title or abbreviation by this Act or another enactment.

(8) Subsection (7) does not apply to a person who uses the title "doctor", "surgeon", "pathologist" or "oncologist" or the abbreviation "Dr." alone or in combination with other words in connection with teaching, research or administration.

(9) No person shall use the word "nurse" alone or in combination with other words that in a manner states or implies that the person is a regulated member unless the person is authorized to use the word pursuant to Schedule 10, 24 or 25 or another enactment.

(10) No person or group of persons shall use the word "registered" or "regulated" or the phrase "regulated health professional" alone or in combination with other words that in a manner states or implies that the person is a regulated member unless the person or group of persons

    (a) is a regulated member or consists of a group of regulated members, or

(b) is a person or group of persons authorized to use the word "registered" or "regulated" or the phrase "regulated health professional" in connection with the health service by another enactment.

(11) No regulated member shall use the term "specialist" or hold himself or herself out to be a specialist in connection with providing a health service unless the regulated member is authorized to use the term "specialist" by a Schedule to this Act or by a regulation made under section 131 or by a bylaw made under section 132 or as otherwise authorized by a council.

Health Professions Act
c. H-7, Schedule 23 Profession of Registered Dietitians and Registered Nutritionists

s. 2. A regulated member of the College of Dietitians of Alberta may, as authorized by the regulations, use any of the following titles, abbreviations and initials:

(a) registered dietitian;

(b) dietitian;

(c) registered nutritionist;

(d) repealed 2001 c21 s45;

(e) R.D.

British Columbia

As this is being written, British Columbia is in the process of making the transition to a Restricted Activities regulatory model similar to that of Alberta and Ontario. The *Health Professions Act* implementing this change received royal assent in 2003, so this process has been under way for several years and is nearly complete. There are currently twenty-five self-regulating professions governed by twenty regulatory colleges under the *Health Professions Act*. One aspect of the transition B.C. has yet to fully implement is the list of Restricted Activities that may only be performed by members of a Regulated Health Profession. The most recent draft of the proposed Restricted Activities was published for discussion in March 2010 and provides us with an indication of what changes may be in store for Holistic Nutritionists in B.C. I have included the list of proposed Restricted Activities in the legislative summary at the end of this section.

Until the Restricted Activities are adopted under the *Health Professions Act*, the rules that impact the practices of Holistic Nutritionists in B.C. are primarily found in the *Medical Practitioners Regulation, Naturopathic Physicians Regulation* and the *Dietitians Regulation*.

The *Medical Practitioners Regulation* stipulates that only a registrant under the regulation (i.e., a medical practitioner) may provide a service of Medicine, if that service was previously restricted under the old *Medical Practitioners Act* (which was repealed by the *Health Professions Act*). This regulation also sets out certain actions that are deemed to be the practice of Medicine. These include, among other things, the assessment and management of a physical or mental condition, the prevention and treatment of physical and mental diseases and the promotion of good health.

The good news for Holistic Nutritionists is that the old rules restricted only the practice of traditional areas of Medicine, such as diagnosing and prescribing treatments for diseases and disorders and did not restrict activities such as disease prevention and the promotion of good health. So Holistic Nutritionists are not currently prohibited from assisting clients to prevent disease or improve health.

The *Naturopathic Physicians Regulation* defines the scope of Naturopathic Medicine and reserves titles such as "Naturopath" for exclusive use by registered Naturopaths. It does not however, in any way, restrict an unregistered person from carrying on the practice of a Naturopath.

The *Dietitians Regulation* defines the scope of a registered a Dietitian's practice. It also identifies certain practices which may only be performed by qualified registered Dietititans. These include designing therapeutic diets that are to be administered by enteral or parenteral means, compounding and dispensing diets that are to be administered by enteral means, and administering substances by instillation through enteral or parenteral means.

The *Dietitians Regulation* reserves the title "Dietitian" for the exclusive use of registered Dietitians. The *Health Professions Act* provides that where a title is reserved for the exclusive use by a Regulated Health Profession, no one other than a lawful registrant (i.e., a member of the appropriate college) may use the title, an abbreviation of the title or an equivalent of the title or abbreviation in another language. As the Act does not restrict in any way the use of the title "Nutritionist," use of this title in B.C. is not restricted.

At the present time, a Holistic Nutritionist who is not a member of a Regulated Health Profession in B.C. may carry on a conventional nutritional practice provided he or she: (1) does not provide the service of "Medicine" as this term is defined in the Medical Practitioners Regulation; (2) does not market themselves to the public using a title reserved for registered Dietitians, Medical Doctors, Naturopaths or any another Regulated Health Profession or otherwise falsely represent themselves as being a registered Dietitian, Medical Doctor, Naturopath, etc.; and (3) otherwise complies with laws of general application.

It must be remembered that the broad restriction contained in the *Medical Practitioner's Regulation* is to be replaced by a list of Restricted Activities. Once the regulation implementing the Restricted Activities is adopted, a Holistic Nutritionist in B.C. will not be able to perform any of these procedures unless he or she is also a member of a Regulated Health Profession who has been authorized to do so. If the list does not change from the current proposal,[16] activities such as diagnosing diseases and prescribing and dispensing drugs will be restricted, but not administering a treatment, unless in doing so another Restricted Activity is performed. So, once the Restricted Activities are adopted, and assuming no changes are made to what is currently being proposed, a Holistic Nutritionist will be permitted, for example, to treat a disease that has been diagnosed by a medical doctor or self-diagnosed by the client by recommending dietary changes, food supplements and natural health products.

For a better understanding of how terms such as "diagnose" and "treat," etc. are to be interpreted, the reader should review the discussion of terminology in the next chapter.

---

[16] As the regulations establishing the Registered Health Professions (for example the *Dietitians Regulation*) are incorporating into their provisions many of the Restricted Activities from this list, it would appear unlikely, although not certain, that major changes will be made prior to implementation.

Restrictions on Activities in British Columbia

The Medical Practitioners Regulation
B.C. Reg. 416/2008

s.1 In this regulation:

"medicine" means the health profession in which a person provides the services of

(a) assessment and management of the physical or mental condition of an individual or group of individuals at any stage of the biological life cycle, including the prenatal and postmortem periods,

(b) prevention and treatment of physical and mental diseases, disorders and conditions, and

(c) promotion of good health;

Restricted activities

s. 4 (1) A registrant in the course of practising medicine may perform any restricted activity.

(2) Only a registrant may provide a service of medicine as set out in this regulation if, on the day before this section comes into force, the provision of the same service by anyone other than a person authorized under the Medical Practitioners Act was prohibited.

The Dietitians Regulation
B.C. Reg. 279/2008

s. 1 In this regulation:

"Act" means the Health Professions Act;

"compound" means to mix ingredients for parenteral or enteral nutrition;

"dietetics" means the assessment of nutritional needs, design, implementation and evaluation of nutritional care plans and therapeutic diets, the science of food and human nutrition, and dissemination of information about food and human nutrition to attain, maintain and promote the health of individuals, groups and the community;

"design" means the selection of appropriate ingredients for parenteral or enteral nutrition;

"dispense" means to fill a prescription for parenteral or enteral nutrition;

"enteral" means administration of a nutritional substance to a patient by means of a feeding tube into the gastrointestinal tract;

"parenteral" means administration of a nutritional substance to a patient directly into the blood stream.

Restricted activities

s.5 No person other than a registrant who meets the additional qualifications set out in the bylaws of the college may

    (a) design, compound or dispense therapeutic diets if nutrition is administered through enteral means,

    (b) design therapeutic diets if nutrition is administered through parenteral means, or

    (c) administer a substance to a person by instillation through enteral or parenteral means.

Proposed List of Restricted Activities, March 2010
Current draft of proposed Restricted Activities which are to be enacted on a date to be determined

1. Making a diagnosis identifying a disease, disorder or condition as the cause of signs or symptoms of the individual.
2. Performing the following physically invasive or physically manipulative acts:
    a. procedures on tissue below the dermis, below the surface of a mucous membrane, in or below the surface of the cornea, in or below the surfaces of the teeth, including the scaling of teeth;
    b. setting or casting a fracture of a bone or reducing a dislocation of a joint;
    c. movement of the joints of the spine beyond the limits the body can voluntarily achieve but within the anatomical range of motion using a high velocity, low amplitude thrust;
    d. administering a substance, other than a drug,
        i. by injection,
        ii. by inhalation,
        iii. by mechanical ventilation
        iv. by irrigation, or
        v. by instillation through enteral or parenteral means; and
    e. putting an instrument, hand or finger(s),
        i. into the external ear canal, including applying pressurized air or water,
        ii. beyond the point in the nasal passages, where they normally narrow,
        iii. beyond the pharynx,
        iv. beyond the opening of the urethra,
        v. beyond the labia majora,
        vi. beyond the anal verge, or
        vii. into an artificial opening into the body.
3. Managing labour or delivery of a baby.

4. Applying or ordering the application of a hazardous form of energy including diagnostic ultrasound, electricity, magnetic resonance imaging, lithotripsy, laser and X-ray, or as prescribed by regulation.

5.
   a. Prescribing, compounding, dispensing or administering by any means a drug listed in Schedule I or II of the Pharmacists, Pharmacy Operations and Drug Scheduling Act.

      For the purposes of this reserved act, the following definitions shall apply:

      "prescribing": the ordering of a drug.

      "compounding": mixing ingredients, at least one of which is a drug.

      "dispensing": preparing or filling a prescription for drugs.

   b. Designing, compounding or dispensing therapeutic diets where nutrition is administered through enteral or parenteral means.

      For the purposes of this reserved act, the following definitions shall apply:

      "designing": the selection of appropriate ingredients for enteral or parenteral nutrition.

      "compounding": mixing ingredients, for enteral or parenteral nutrition

      "dispensing": filling a prescription for enteral or parenteral nutrition.

6. Prescribing appliances or devices for vision, hearing or dental conditions; dispensing such prescribed appliances or devices for dental conditions; fitting such appliances or devices for dental conditions, or fitting contact lenses.

For the purposes of this reserved act, the following definitions shall apply:

"prescribing": ordering the fabrication or alteration of appliances or devices for vision, hearing, or dental conditions.

"dispensing": filling a prescription by fabricating or altering a dental appliance or device.

   a. Allergy challenge testing or allergy desensitizing treatment involving injection, scratch tests or inhalation, and allergy challenge testing by any means with respect to a patient who has had a previous anaphylactic reaction;

   b. Cardiac stress testing conducted for medical diagnosis and treatment planning.

Restrictions on Professional Titles in British Columbia

Dietitians Regulation
B.C. Reg. 279/2008

s. 3 The title "dietitian" is reserved for exclusive use by registrants

Health Professions Act
RSBC 1996 C. 183

s.12.1 (1) If a regulation under section 12 (2) (b) prescribes a title to be used exclusively by registrants of a college, a person other than a registrant of the college must not use the title, an abbreviation of the title or an equivalent of the title or abbreviation in another language

      (a) to describe the person's work,

      (b) in association with or as part of another title describing the person's work, or

      (c) in association with a description of the person's work.

(2) If a regulation under section 12 (2) (b.1) prescribes a limit or condition respecting the use of a title, the title must not be used except in accordance with the regulation.

(3) A person other than a registrant of a college must not use a name, title, description or abbreviation of a name or title, or an equivalent of a name or title in another language, in any manner that expresses or implies that he or she is a registrant or associated with the college.

Manitoba

As this is being written, the province of Manitoba is in the process of making the transition to a Restricted Activities regulatory approach similar to that of Alberta and Ontario. The provincial *Regulated Health Professions Act* received royal assent on June 11, 2009 and is to come into force on a date which is still to be set. Based on experiences in other provinces, it will likely take several years for the government to promulgate the necessary regulations and for the existing Regulated Health Professions to update their governance and other procedures to conform to the statute. I will provide a short summary of the current rules, as well as the rules as they will exist once the *Regulated Health Professions Act* is in force.

PART A - Current Legislation

Until the new *Regulated Health Professions Act* is proclaimed into force, the rules that impact the practices of Holistic Nutritionists in Manitoba are primarily found in The *Medical Act* and The *Registered Dietitians Act*.

The *Medical Act* makes it an offence to practice Medicine or to hold oneself out as being qualified to practice Medicine unless licensed to do so under the Act. The *Medical Act* also sets out certain acts, the practice of which is deemed to be the practice of Medicine. These include, among other things, diagnosing and treating diseases, ailments, defects, etc. This is not an exhaustive list, however, so the question of whether in providing services a Holistic Nutritionist is practising Medicine would ultimately be determined by the Courts.

The *Naturopathic Act* makes it an offence to practice naturopathy or use the title "Naturopath" unless authorized to do so under the Act. The *Naturopathic Act* also defines the practice of Naturopathy to be "a drugless system of therapy that treats human injuries, ailments, or diseases, by natural methods . . .". Since the treatment of "injuries, ailments, or diseases" etc. by any method is already restricted by the *Medical Act*, this restriction in the *Naturopathic Act* does not further limit the area of practice that is presently open to Holistic Nutritionists in Manitoba.

The *Registered Dietitians Act* defines the scope of a registered Dietitian's practice. While it does not restrict an unregulated professional from carrying on a Dietitian's practice, it does makes it unlawful to wrongfully imply one is a registered Dietitian entitled to engage in the practice of Dietetics.

The *Registered Dietitians Act* reserves the title "Dietitian" and several related variations for the exclusive use of registered Dietitians. It also prohibits anyone who is not a registered Dietitian from using any title, etc. that implies he or she is a registered Dietitian. As the Act does not restrict in any way the use of the title "Nutritionist," Holistic Nutritionists may use this word as part of professional title or in their advertising and marketing materials.

A Holistic Nutritionist who is not a member of a Regulated Health Profession in Manitoba may carry on a conventional nutritional practice provided he or she: (1) does not "practice Medicine" as this term is defined in the *Medical Act* and has been interpreted by the Courts; (2) does not practice Naturopathy as defined in the *Naturopathic Act*; (3) does not market themselves to the public using a title reserved for Registered Dietitians, Medical Doctors or Naturopaths, or any another Regulated Health Profession or otherwise falsely represent themselves as being a registered Dietitian, etc.; and (4) otherwise complies with laws of general application.

For a better understanding of how terms such as "practice of Medicine," "diagnose" and "treat," etc. are to be interpreted, the reader should review the discussion of terminology in the next chapter.

PART B – New Regulated Health Professions Act

As noted above, sometime in the next several years the current rules governing Regulated Health Professions in the Province of Manitoba will be replaced by the *Regulated Health Professions Act*. The date for this change has not yet been determined.

The *Regulated Health Professions Act* will establish the various Regulated Health Professions and the rules that will apply to their operation as self-governing professions. The Act will also establish "Reserved Acts" (i.e., Restricted Activities) that may only be performed by members of Regulated Health Professions. Once this Act is in force, a person who is not a member of a Regulated Health Profession will not be able to perform any of these procedures.

Assuming the rules are not further amended before coming into force, a Holistic Nutritionist in Manitoba who is not a member of a Regulated Health Profession will be able carry on a conventional nutritional practice provided he or she: (1) does not perform a Reserved Act described in the *Regulated Health Professions Act*; (2) does not market themselves to the public using a title reserved for Registered Dietitians or any another Regulated Health Profession or otherwise falsely represent themselves as being a registered Dietitian, etc.; and (3) otherwise complies with laws of general application.

I have set out, on the following pages, the list of Reserved Acts in its entirety. In reviewing the Reserved Acts, the reader will see that while the diagnosis of diseases, etc. will continue to be a Restricted Activity in Manitoba, the treatment of diseases, etc. per se will not be, provided the treatment does not involve one of the Reserved Acts (e.g., prescribing drugs). So, once the *Regulated Health Professions Act* is proclaimed into force, a Holistic Nutritionist will be permitted, for example, to treat a disease that has been diagnosed by a medical doctor or self-diagnosed by the client by recommending dietary changes, food supplements and natural health products.

The new rules will not alter the rules surrounding the titles a Holistic Nutritionist may use in the province of Manitoba.

PART A - Current Legislation
(To be replaced the Regulated Health Professions Act on a date yet to be determined)

Restrictions on Activities in Manitoba

The Medical Act
C.C.S.M. c. M90

s. 2(1) Without restricting the generality of the definition of practice of medicine, a person shall be deemed to be practising medicine within the meaning of this Act who

(a) by advertisement, sign, or statement of any kind, written or oral, alleges or implies or states that he is, or holds himself out as being, qualified, able, or willing, to diagnose, prescribe for, prevent, or treat, any human disease, ailment, deformity, defect, or injury, or to perform any operation or surgery to remedy any human disease, ailment, deformity, defect, or injury, or to examine or advise upon the physical or mental condition of any person; or

(b) diagnoses, or offers to diagnose, or attempts by any means whatsoever to diagnose, any human disease, ailment, deformity, defect, or injury, or who examines or advises upon, or offers to examine or advise upon, the physical or mental condition of any person; or

(c) prescribes or administers any drugs, serum, medicine, or any substance or remedy, whether for the cure, treatment, or prevention, of any human disease, ailment, deformity, defect, or injury; or

(d) prescribes or administers any treatment, or performs any operation or manipulation, or applies any apparatus or appliance, for the cure, treatment, or prevention, of any human disease, ailment, deformity, defect, or injury, or acts as a midwife; or

(e) repealed, S.M. 1999, c. 39, s. 3.

s. 66(2) Any person not licensed under this Act who practises or professes to practise medicine in the province, is guilty of an offence.

The Registered Dietitians Act,
C.C.S.M. c. R39

s. 2 The practice of dietetics means the translation and application of scientific knowledge of foods and human nutrition through

(a) assessment, design, implementation and evaluation of nutritional interventions;

(b) integration of food and nutrition principles in the management of food service systems; and

(c) dissemination of information to attain, maintain, promote and protect the health of individuals, groups and the community.

Representation as a registered dietitian or dietitian

s. 3(1)   No person except a registered dietitian shall

(a) represent or hold out, expressly or by implication, that he or she is a registered dietitian or a dietitian, or is entitled to engage in the practice of dietetics as a registered dietitian or as a dietitian; or

(b) use any sign, display, title or advertisement implying that he or she is a registered dietitian or a dietitian.

Restriction on Professional Titles in Manitoba

The Registered Dietitians Act
C.C.S.M. c. R39

s. 3(2) No person except a registered dietitian shall use the title "registered dietitian" or "dietitian", a variation or abbreviation of either title, or an equivalent of either title in another language.

Use of title "graduate dietitian"

s. 3(3) Unless authorized by the council, no person except a graduate dietitian shall use the title "graduate dietitian", a variation or abbreviation of that title, or an equivalent in another language.

Use of title "dietetic intern"

s. 3(4) Unless authorized by the council, no person except a person enrolled in a dietetic education program referred to in subclause 9(2)(a)(i) shall use the title "dietetic intern", a variation or abbreviation of that title, or an equivalent in another.

PART B – The Regulated Health Professions Act
(To be proclaimed into force, and replace the current legislation on a date to be determined)

Proposed Restrictions on Activities in Manitoba

List of reserved acts

s. 4 A "reserved act" is any of the following acts done with respect to an individual in the course of providing health care:

1. Making a diagnosis and communicating it to an individual or his or her personal representative in circumstances in which it is reasonably foreseeable that the individual or representative will rely on the diagnosis to make a decision about the individual's health care.

2. Ordering or receiving reports of screening or diagnostic tests.

3. Performing a procedure on tissue

   (a) below the dermis;

   (b) below the surface of a mucous membrane;

   (c) on or below the surface of the cornea; or

   (d) on or below the surface of a tooth or dental implant, including the scaling of a tooth or dental implant.

4. Inserting or removing an instrument or a device, hand or finger

   (a) into the external ear canal;

   (b) beyond the point in the nasal passages where they normally narrow;

   (c) beyond the pharynx;

   (d) beyond the opening of the urethra;

   (e) beyond the labia majora;

   (f) beyond the anal verge; or

   (g) into an artificial opening in the body.

5. Administering a substance

   (a) by injection;

   (b) by inhalation;

   (c) by mechanical ventilation;

   (d) by irrigation;

   (e) by enteral instillation or parenteral instillation;

(f) by transfusion; or

(g) using a hyperbaric chamber.

6. Prescribing a drug or vaccine.

7. Compounding a drug or vaccine.

8. Dispensing or selling a drug or vaccine.

9. Administering a drug or vaccine by any method.

10. Applying or ordering the application of

(a) ultrasound for diagnostic or imaging purposes, including any application of ultrasound to a fetus;

(b) electricity for

(i) aversive conditioning,

(ii) cardiac pacemaker therapy,

(iii) cardioversion,

(iv) defibrillation,

(v) electrocoagulation,

(vi) electroconvulsive shock therapy,

(vii) electromyography,

(viii) fulguration,

(ix) nerve conduction studies, or

(x) transcutaneous cardiac pacing;

(c) electromagnetism for magnetic resonance imaging;

(d) other non-ionizing radiation for the purpose of cutting or destroying tissue or medical imagery;

(e) X-rays or other ionizing radiation for diagnostic, imaging or therapeutic purposes, including computerized axial tomography, positron emission tomography and radiation therapy;

(f) any other use of a form of energy listed in clauses (a) to (e), if the use is specified by regulation; or

(g) any other form of energy that is specified by regulation.

11. In relation to a therapeutic diet that is administered by enteral instillation or parenteral instillation,

(a) selecting ingredients for the diet; or

(b) compounding or administering the diet.

12. Setting or casting a fracture of a bone or a dislocation of a joint.

13. Putting into the external ear canal, up to the eardrum, a substance that

(a) is under pressure; or

(b) subsequently solidifies.

14. Managing labour or the delivery of a baby.

15. Administering a high velocity, low amplitude thrust to move a joint of the spine within its anatomical range of motion.

16. Prescribing, dispensing or fitting a wearable hearing instrument.

17. Prescribing, dispensing or verifying a vision appliance.

18. Fitting a contact lens.

19. Prescribing, dispensing or fitting a dental appliance.

20. Performing a psycho-social intervention with an expectation of modifying a substantial disorder of thought, mood, perception, orientation or memory that grossly impairs judgment, behaviour, the capacity to recognize reality, or the ability to meet the ordinary demands of life.

21. In relation to allergies,

(a) performing challenge testing by any method; or

(b) performing desensitizing treatment by any method.

New Brunswick

The rules that impact the practices of Holistic Nutritionists in New Brunswick are primarily found in the *Medical Act* and *An Act Respecting the New Brunswick Association of Dietitians* (the *"Dietitians Act"*). Naturopathy is not a regulated profession in New Brunswick.

The *Medical Act* makes it an offence to practice or hold oneself out to be able to practice Medicine, unless licensed to do so under the Act. The *Medical Act* also provides an illustrative list of practice areas (Medicine, surgery, and osteopathic Medicine and the specialties and subspecialties thereof) that are deemed to be included within the meaning of "Medicine." As the definition of the practice of Medicine in the Act does not include any defined activities, the question of whether in providing services a Holistic Nutritionist is practising Medicine would be determined by the Courts, although practising Medicine is generally interpreted to include, among other things, diagnosing and treating diseases and disorders.

The *Dietitians Act* expansively defines the practice area of a Registered Dietitian and prohibits unregistered persons from providing such services to the public. For example, this Act defines the practice of Dietetics to mean "the translation and application of the scientific knowledge of foods and human nutrition towards the attainment, maintenance and promotion of the health of individuals" and includes within this "assessing nutritional needs of individuals and developing and implementing nutritional care plans based on the assessments" and "establishing and reviewing the principles of nutrition and guidelines for healthy and ill people throughout their lives." Unless one is a Registered Dietitian (or a member of another Regulated Health Profession whose practice area includes nutritional counselling, such as a medical doctor) not only must one avoid treating diseases and disorders nutritionally, one must avoid the business of performing assessments and providing advice to individuals that promotes wellness.

This *Dietitians Act* also reserves the titles "Dietitian" and "Registered Dietitian-Nutritionist," among others, for exclusive use by Registered Dietitians. As the Act does not reserve use of the word "Nutritionist" on its own, the use of the word "Nutritionist" either on its own or in combination with other words other than as part of the phrase "Registered Dietitian – Nutritionist" (for example "Holistic Nutritionist") is not strictly speaking prohibited. However, since the Act also restricts the use of other designations that "represent" the restricted title, the use of "Nutritionist" as part of a professional title should be avoided.

As a result of the rules contained in the *Medical Act* and the *Dietitians Act*, I do not believe it is possible for a Holistic Nutritionist to lawfully carry on a conventional nutritional counselling practice in the province of New Brunswick.

For a better understanding of how terms such as "practice of Medicine" are to be interpreted, the reader should review the discussion of terminology in the next chapter.

Restrictions on Activities in New Brunswick

The Medical Act, 1981

s. 3 "**practice of medicine**" includes the practice of medicine, surgery, and osteopathic medicine and the specialties and subspecialties thereof;

s. 43(1) A person licensed under this Act who practices medicine in violation of any condition or limitation contained in his licence commits an offence 43(2) A person who practices medicine

> (a) while his licence is suspended or revoked, or
>
> (b) without a licence, commits an offence.

s. 45(1) Except as provided in this Act and the regulations, no person, other than a medical practitioner who holds a licence or a professional corporation which holds a licence shall

> (a) publicly or privately, for hire, gain or hope of reward, practise or offer to practise medicine;
>
> (b) hold himself out in any way to be entitled to practise medicine; or
>
> (c) use any title or description implying or designed to lead the public to believe that he is entitled to practise medicine.

An Act Respecting the New Brunswick Association of Dietitians
C. 75 1988

s. 2 "practice of dietetics" means the translation and application of the scientific knowledge of foods and human nutrition towards the attainment, maintenance and promotion of the health of individuals, groups and the community and includes the following:

> (a) administering food service systems though this function is not exclusive to dietitians;
>
> (b) assessing nutritional needs of individuals and developing and implementing nutritional care plans based on the assessments;
>
> (c) establishing and reviewing the principles of nutrition and guidelines for healthy and ill people throughout their lives;

(d) assessing the overall nutritional needs of a community in order to establish priorities and to influence policies which provide the nutritional component of preventative programs, and implementing and evaluating those programs;

(e) interpreting and evaluating, for consumer protection, information on nutrition that is available to the public;

(f) consulting with individuals, families and groups on the principles of food and nutrition and the practical application of those principles;

(g) planning, conducting and evaluating educational programs on nutrition;

(h) conducting basic and applied research in food, nutrition and food service systems though this function is not exclusive to dietitians;

"registered dietitian" means a person who holds an annual certificate as a registered dietitian under this Act;

12(2) Except as provided in this Act, the by-laws or regulations no person shall engage in or hold herself out as engaging in the practice of dietetics unless she is registered under this Act.

Restrictions on Professional Titles in New Brunswick

An Act Respecting the New Brunswick Association of Dietitians
C. 75 1988

12(3) Except as provided in this Act, the by-laws or regulations no person shall use the title "Dietitian", "Dietician", "Professional Dietitian", "Registered Dietitian - Nutritionist", "Registered Dietitian", or the abbreviations "P.Dt.", "R.D." or "RON" or other designation representing the title, unless such person is a registered dietitian.

Newfoundland and Labrador

The rules that impact the practices of Holistic Nutritionists in Newfoundland and Labrador are primarily found in the *Medical Act* and the *Dietitians Act*.

The *Medical Act* makes it an offence to practice or to hold oneself out as being qualified to practice Medicine, unless licensed to do so under the Act. The *Medical Act* also contains an illustrative list of practice areas (e.g., cardiology, dermatology) that are deemed to be included within the meaning of "Medicine." As the definition of the practice of Medicine in the Act does not include any defined activities, the question of whether in providing services a Holistic Nutritionist is practising Medicine would be determined by the Courts, although practising Medicine is generally interpreted to include, among other things, diagnosing and treating diseases and disorders.

The *Dietitians Act* does not define the practice of Dietetics or grant exclusive rights to practise to Registered Dietitians. As a result, the Act does not restrict the practice of a Holistic Nutritionist. The *Dietitians Act* does, however, reserve the title "Dietitian" and several related variations for the exclusive use of registered Dietitians. It also prohibits anyone who is not a registered Dietitian from implying he or she is a registered Dietitian. As the Act does not restrict in any way the use of the title "Nutritionist" Holistic Nutritionists may use this word as part of professional title or in their advertising and marketing materials.

Naturopathy is not a regulated profession in Newfoundland and Labrador.

As this is being written, the Province of Newfoundland and Labrador is in the process of reforming its regulation of health services by implementing Regulated Health Profession legislation that will serve to bring a standardized regulatory approach to certain health professions while largely preserving the existing rules for many currently regulated Health Professions, such as Medicine and Dietetics. This hybrid approach is unique in Canada. As the new *Health Professions Act* does not impact the regulation of the practice of Medicine or Dietetics, nor expand regulation to include Naturopathy, it is not of immediate interest to Holistic Nutritionists, and therefore, is not summarized.

A Holistic Nutritionist who is not a member of a Regulated Health Profession in Newfoundland and Labrador may carry on a conventional nutritional practice provided he or she: (1) does not practice Medicine as this term has been defined by the Courts; (2) does not market themselves to the public using a title reserved for Registered Dietitians, Medical Doctors or any another Regulated Health Profession or otherwise falsely represent themselves as being a registered Dietitian or Medical Doctor, etc.; and (3) otherwise complies with laws of general application.

For a better understanding of how terms such as "practice of Medicine" are to be interpreted, the reader should review the discussion of terminology in the next chapter.

Restrictions on Activities in Newfoundland and Labrador

Medical Act
SNL 2005 c. M-4.01

s. 2. In this Act

(o) "practice of medicine" means the practice of medicine or surgery on the human body, and includes cardiology, dermatology, geriatrics, gynecology, neurology, obstetrics, ophthalmology, orthopedics, pathology, pediatrics, psychiatry and radiology and other specialities and subspecialties of medicine;

Offence

s. 68. (1) A person, other than a person who is licensed under this Act, shall not

(a) engage in the practice of medicine;

(b) hold himself or herself out or allege by advertisement, sign or statement of any kind to be entitled to engage in the practice of medicine; or

(c) take or use a name, title or description implying or calculated to lead the public to believe that he or she is licensed under this Act.

Restrictions on Professional Titles in Newfoundland and Labrador

Dietitians Act
SNL 2005 c. D-23.1

s. 20. (1) A person who is not a registered dietitian shall not take or use the titles "Dietitian" or "Registered Dietitian" or the initials "R.D." either alone or in combination with other words, letters or description that implies that the person is registered under this Act, or is entitled to be registered under this Act, or is recognized by law as a registered dietitian.

Nova Scotia

The rules that impact the practices of Holistic Nutritionists in Nova Scotia are primarily found in the *Medical Act* and the *Professional Dietitians Act*.

The *Medical Act* makes it an offence to practise Medicine or to hold oneself out as being qualified to practise Medicine *unless* licensed to do so under the Act. The *Medical Act* also sets out certain acts, the practice of which is deemed to be the practice of Medicine. These include, among other things, diagnosing and treating diseases, illnesses, defects, etc.

The *Naturopathic Doctors Act* makes it an offence to practise Naturopathy or use the title "Naturopath," etc. unless authorized to do so under the Act. This Act also defines the practice of Naturopathy to be "the assessment of diseases, disorders and dysfunctions and the naturopathic diagnosis and treatment of diseases, disorders and dysfunctions using naturopathic techniques to promote, maintain or restore health." As the diagnosis and treatment of diseases and disorders by any method is already restricted by the *Medical Act* (as these activities are seen to be within the scope of the practice of Medicine), this restriction in the *Naturopathic Doctors Act* does not further limit the area of practice that is presently available to Holistic Nutritionists in Nova Scotia. Accordingly, I have not included provisions from the Act in the legislative summaries below.

The rules governing the practice of Dietitians, the profession which is closest in nature to Holistic Nutritionists, is currently undergoing change. The existing Act, the *Professional Dietitians Act,* is to be replaced by a new statute, the *Dietitians Act* c. 2 of the Acts of 2009, which received Royal Assent in 2009 but which, as this is being written, has not yet been proclaimed into force. To assist Holistic Nutritionists in Nova Scotia with their planning, both Acts have been summarized.

The current rules do not define the practice of Dietetics or grant exclusive rights to practise to Registered Dietitians. As a result, the current rules do not restrict the practice of a Holistic Nutritionist. The rules do, however, reserve several titles for exclusive use by Registered Dietitians, including "Dietitian" and "Nutritionist" and several variations. As the use of "Nutritionist" is prohibited, Holistic Nutritionists may not use it as part of a professional title in Nova Scotia.

By contrast, the rules in the new *Dietitians Act* both expansively define the practice area of a Registered Dietitian <u>and</u> prohibit unregistered persons from providing such services to the public. For example, the new rules define the practice of Dietetics to include: "planning, implementation and evaluation of nutrition interventions aimed at promoting health and preventing disease" and prohibit anyone from providing this service, unless registered under the new Act. The new rules also include the broad restrictions on professional titles contained in the old rules.

Until the new *Dietitians Act* is proclaimed into force, a Holistic Nutritionist who is not a member of a Regulated Health Profession in Nova Scotia may carry on a conventional nutritional practice provided he or she: (1) does not practice Medicine as this term is defined in the *Medical Act* and has been interpreted by the Courts; (2) does not practice Naturopathy as this term is defined in the *Naturopathic Doctors Act*; (3) does not market themselves to the public using a title reserved for Registered Dietitians, Medical Doctors or Registered Naturopaths or any another Regulated Health Profession or otherwise falsely represent themselves as being a Registered Dietitian, Medical Doctor or Registered Naturopath, etc.; and (4) otherwise complies with laws of general application.

Once the new *Dietitians Act* is proclaimed into force, it will be virtually impossible for anyone other than a member of the Nova Scotia Dietetics Association to operate a conventional nutritional counselling practice in that province. We will have to see whether this monopoly is actively enforced. However, one wishes the legislature would have heeded the wisdom of Appeals Justice Osler as articulated in *Ontario Medical Act*, R.S.O. 1897, c. 176 when commenting about the scope of the practice of Medicine: "Nevertheless, we cannot say that the profession, wide as have been its conquests and extended the scope of its practice, has taken all knowledge of the art of healing for its province . . .".

For a better understanding of how terms such as "practice of Medicine" are to be interpreted, the reader should review the discussion of terminology in the next chapter.

Restrictions on Activities in Nova Scotia

Medical Act
c. 10 of the Acts of 1995-96

s. 2 In this Act, unless the context otherwise requires,

(w) "practice of medicine" includes, but is not restricted to,

> (i) advertising, holding out to the public or representing in any manner that one is authorized to practise medicine in the jurisdiction,
> (ii) offering or undertaking to prescribe, order, give or administer any drug or medicine for the use of any other person,
> (iii) offering or undertaking to prevent or to diagnose, correct or treat in any

manner or by any means, methods, devices or instrumentalities any disease, illness, pain, wound, fracture, infirmity, defect or abnormal physical or mental condition of any person,

(iv) offering or undertaking to perform any obstetrical procedure or surgical operation upon any person;

s. 38 (2) A person who practises medicine

(a) while the person's licence is suspended or revoked; or

(b) without a licence,

commits an offence. *1995-96, c. 10, s. 38.*

s. 40 (1) Except as provided in this Act and the regulations, no person, other than a medical practitioner who holds a licence shall

(a) publicly or privately, for hire, gain or hope of reward, practise or offer to practise medicine;

(b) hold himself or herself out in any way to be entitled to practise medicine; or

(c) assume any title or description implying or designed to lead the public to believe that that person is entitled to practise medicine.

Professional Dietitians Act
c. 361 of the revised statutes, 1989
(to be replaced by the Dietitians Act c. 2 of the Acts of 2009 on a date to be determined)

No applicable practice restrictions.

The Dietitians Act
c. 2 of the Acts of 2009
(to replace the Professional Dietitians Act on a date to be determined)

s. 2 In this Act,

(x) "practice of dietetics" means the translation and application of scientific knowledge of food and nutrition to human health through

(i) comprehensive nutritional assessment to determine nutritional status, nutrition-related diagnosis and nutritional requirements of individuals or populations related to health status and disease,

(ii) the planning, implementation and evaluation of nutrition interventions aimed at promoting health and preventing disease,

(iii) nutrition prescription, including enteral and parenteral nutrition and the prescription or ordering of drugs or other agents to optimize nutrition status,

(iv) ordering parameters required to monitor nutrition interventions and evaluate nutrition outcomes,

(v) the provision of nutrition education and counselling to clients, families, colleagues and health-care professionals,

(vi) development and evaluation of policies that affect food, food security and nutrition as it relates to health status,

(vii) integration of food and nutrition principles in the development and management of food service systems,

(viii) such delegated medical functions as are approved in accordance with the Medical Act, and

(ix) such other aspects of dietetics as may be prescribed in regulations approved by the Governor in Council, and

(x) research, education, consultation, management, administration, regulation, policy or system development relevant to subclauses (i) to (ix);

(ao) "scope of practice of the profession" means the roles, functions and accountabilities that dietitians are educated and authorized to perform;

s. 21 (1) No person shall engage in the practice of dietetics or describe the person's activities as "dietetics", "nutrition therapy" or "diet therapy" unless such person

(a) holds an active-practising licence with or without restrictions or conditions;

(b) is the holder of a temporary licence with or without restrictions or conditions;

(c) is the holder of a candidate licence with or without restrictions or conditions; or

(d) is otherwise authorized to engage in the practice of dietetics as set out in this Act or the regulations.

(2) No person shall

(a) take or use the designations "Dietitian", "Registered Dietitian", "Nutritionist", "Professional Nutritionist", "Professional Dietitian", "R.D.", "P.Dt", "R.D.N." or any derivation, translation or abbreviation thereof; or

(b) describe the person's activities as "Dietetics", "Nutrition Therapy" or "Diet Therapy",

in the Province, either alone or in combination with other words, letters or descriptions to imply that the person is entitled to practise as a dietitian unless the person

(c) holds an active-practising licence with or without restrictions or conditions;

(d) is the holder of a temporary licence with or without restrictions or conditions; or

(e) is otherwise authorized to use such designation and to engage in the practice of dietetics as set out in this Act or the regulations.

(3) No person shall engage in the practice of dietetics or take or use the designation "Dietetic Intern" or any derivation, translation or abbreviation thereof unless the person is

engaged in a practicum approved by the Board and is authorized by the administrators of the practicum or otherwise authorized pursuant to the regulations to engage in the practice of dietetics.

(4) No person shall engage in the practice of dietetics or take or use the designation "Candidate Dietitian" or any derivation, translation or abbreviation thereof unless the person meets the criteria for the issuing of a candidate licence pursuant to this Act and the regulations and is authorized pursuant to the regulations to engage in the practice of dietetics.

(5) In any advertisement or publication, including business cards, websites or signage, no person shall take or use the designation "Registered Dietitian", "Dietitian", "Professional Nutritionist", "Nutritionist", "Dietetic Intern", "Candidate Dietitian" or any derivation, translation or abbreviation thereof, or shall describe the person's activities as "dietetics", "nutrition therapy" or "diet therapy" unless the referenced activity falls within the definition of the "practice of dietetics".

s. 22 (1) No dietitian shall engage in the practice of dietetics that falls outside that dietitian's individual scope of practice.

(2) Unless otherwise authorized pursuant to this Act or the regulations, or any other law, no dietitian shall practise outside the scope of practice of the profession.

Restrictions on Professional Titles in Nova Scotia

Professional Dietitians Act
c. 361 of the revised statutes, 1989
(to be replaced by the Dietitians Act c. 2
of the Acts of 2009 on a date to be determined)

Designation of professional dietitian

s. 12 (2) A person not licensed under this Act who is not qualified for membership in the Association may not use any of the following titles or designations: "Dietitian" or "Dietician", "Dietitian-Nutritionist", "Nutritionist", "Professional Dietitian" or "Professional Dietician", "Professional Dietitian-Nutritionist", "Professional Nutritionist", "Dietetiste", "Dietetiste- Nutritionniste", "Dietetiste Professionelle", "Dieteticienne", "Nutritionniste" or the initials "P.Dt." or "Dt.P." either alone or in combination with other words, letters or descriptions.

Ontario

The provision of health services in Ontario is regulated primarily through the *Regulated Health Professions Act*, its regulations and the associated individual acts that create the various self-governing health professions.

The *Regulated Health Professions Act* establishes the Restricted Activities that may only be performed by members of a Regulated Health Profession. A person who is not a member of a Regulated Health Profession may not perform any of these procedures. In addition, s. 30 of the Act further prohibits anyone from treating or advising a person "in circumstances in which it is reasonably foreseeable that serious bodily harm may result from the treatment or advice or from an omission from them." The Ontario *Medicine Act* also includes a general prohibition against a person who is not a member of the College of Physicians and Surgeons, holding himself/herself out to be a person who is qualified to practise as an osteopath, physician or surgeon or in a specialty of medicine.

While the Ontario *Dietetics Act* does include a short definition of the practice of Dietetics, it does not restrict, in any way, who may engage in such a practice. Which makes sense, as Ontario regulates the provision of health services through Restricted Activities. It does, however, reserve the title "Dietitian" for exclusive use by Registered Dietitians. As the use of the word "Nutritionist" is not in any way restricted in Ontario, Holistic Nutritionists may use it as part of a professional title or in their advertising and marketing materials.

A Holistic Nutritionist in Ontario who is not a member of a Regulated Health Profession may carry on a conventional nutritional counselling practice provided he or she: (1) does not perform any of the Restricted Activities described in the *Regulated Health Professions Act* (see below); (2) does not provide advice or treatment where it is reasonably foreseeable serious bodily harm may result; (3) does not market themselves to the public using a title reserved for Registered Dietitians, Medical Doctors, Naturopaths or any another Regulated Health Profession; and (4) otherwise complies with laws of general application.

I have set out, on the following pages, the list of Restricted Activities in its entirety. In reviewing the Restricted Activities, the reader will see that while the diagnosis of diseases and disorders in situations where it is reasonably foreseeable the individual will rely on the diagnosis is a Restricted Activity, the treatment of diseases and disorders per se is not, provided of course the treatment does not involve a Restricted Activity (e.g., selling or compounding a drug) or pose a serious foreseeable risk of bodily harm. So a Holistic Nutritionist is permitted, for example, to treat a disease or disorder that has been diagnosed by a medical doctor or self-diagnosed by the client by recommending dietary changes, food supplements and natural health products.

For a better understanding of how terms such as "diagnose" are to be interpreted, the reader should review the discussion of terminology in the next chapter.

Restrictions on Activities in Ontario

Regulated Health Professions Act
1991 S.O. 1991, c. 18

Controlled acts restricted

s. 27. (1) No person shall perform a controlled act set out in subsection (2) in the course of providing health care services to an individual unless,

(a) the person is a member authorized by a health profession Act to perform the controlled act; or

(b) the performance of the controlled act has been delegated to the person by a member described in clause (a). 1991, c. 18, s. 27 (1); 1998, c. 18, Sched. G, s. 6.

Controlled acts

(2) A "controlled act" is any one of the following done with respect to an individual:

1. Communicating to the individual or his or her personal representative a diagnosis identifying a disease or disorder as the cause of symptoms of the individual in circumstances in which it is reasonably foreseeable that the individual or his or her personal representative will rely on the diagnosis.

2. Performing a procedure on tissue below the dermis, below the surface of a mucous membrane, in or below the surface of the cornea, or in or below the surfaces of the teeth, including the scaling of teeth.

3. Setting or casting a fracture of a bone or a dislocation of a joint.

4. Moving the joints of the spine beyond the individual's usual physiological range of motion using a fast, low amplitude thrust.

5. Administering a substance by injection or inhalation.

6. Putting an instrument, hand or finger,

    i. beyond the external ear canal,

    ii. beyond the point in the nasal passages where they normally narrow,

    iii. beyond the larynx,

    iv. beyond the opening of the urethra,

    v. beyond the labia majora,

    vi. beyond the anal verge, or

    vii. into an artificial opening into the body.

7. Applying or ordering the application of a form of energy prescribed by the regulations under this Act.

8. Prescribing, dispensing, selling or compounding a drug as defined in the *Drug and Pharmacies Regulation Act*[17], or supervising the part of a pharmacy where such drugs are kept.

9. Prescribing or dispensing, for vision or eye problems, subnormal vision devices, contact lenses or eye glasses other than simple magnifiers.

10. Prescribing a hearing aid for a hearing impaired person.

11. Fitting or dispensing a dental prosthesis, orthodontic or periodontal appliance or a device used inside the mouth to protect teeth from abnormal functioning.

12. Managing labour or conducting the delivery of a baby.

13. Allergy challenge testing of a kind in which a positive result of the test is a significant allergic response. 1991, c. 18, s. 27 (2); 2007, c. 10, Sched. L, s. 32.

Note: On a day to be named by proclamation of the Lieutenant Governor, subsection (2) is amended by the Statutes of Ontario, 2007, chapter 10, Schedule R, subsection 19 (1) by adding the following paragraph:

14. Treating, by means of psychotherapy technique, delivered through a therapeutic relationship, an individual's serious disorder of thought, cognition, mood, emotional regulation, perception or memory that may seriously impair the individual's judgement, insight, behaviour, communication or social functioning.

Treatment, etc., where risk of harm

s. 30. (1) No person, other than a member treating or advising within the scope of practice of his or her profession, shall treat or advise a person with respect to his or her health in circumstances in which it is reasonably foreseeable that serious bodily harm may result from the treatment or advice or from an omission from them. 1991, c. 18, s. 30 (1); 2007, c. 10, Sched. M, s. 6.

Exception

(2) Subsection (1) does not apply with respect to treatment by a person who is acting under the direction of or in collaboration with a member if the treatment is within the scope of practice of the member's profession. 1991, c. 18, s. 30 (2).

Delegation

(3) Subsection (1) does not apply with respect to an act by a person if the act is a controlled act that was delegated under section 28 to the person by a member authorized by a health profession Act to do the controlled act. 1991, c. 18, s. 30 (3).

Counselling

---

[17] Natural Health Products, as defined in the *Natural Health Products Regulations* to Canada's *Food and Drug Act* are not considered drugs under the *Drug and Pharmacies Regulation Act*.

(4) Subsection (1) does not apply with respect to counselling about emotional, social, educational or spiritual matters. 1991, c. 18, s. 30 (4).

Exceptions

(5) Subsection (1) does not apply with respect to anything done by a person in the course of,

> (a) rendering first aid or temporary assistance in an emergency;
>
> (b) fulfilling the requirements to become a member of a health profession if the person is acting within the scope of practice of the profession under the supervision or direction of a member of the profession;
>
> (c) treating a person by prayer or spiritual means in accordance with the tenets of the religion of the person giving the treatment;
>
> (d) treating a member of the person's household; or
>
> (e) assisting a person with his or her routine activities of living. 1991, c. 18, s. 30 (5).

Exemption

(6) Subsection (1) does not apply with respect to an activity or person that is exempted by the regulations. 1991, c. 18, s. 30 (6).

Medicine Act
1991 S.O. 1991, c. 30

Representations of qualification, etc.

s. 9 (3) No person other than a member shall hold himself or herself out as a person who is qualified to practise in Ontario as an osteopath, physician or surgeon or in a specialty of medicine. 1991, c. 30, s. 9 (3).

Restrictions on Professional Titles in Ontario

Dietetics Act
1991 S.O. 1991, c. 26

s. 3 The practice of dietetics is the assessment of nutrition and nutritional conditions and the treatment and prevention of nutrition related disorders by nutritional means.

Restricted titles

s. 7 (1) No person other than a member shall use the title "dietitian", a variation or abbreviation or an equivalent in another language. 1991, c. 26, s. 7 (1).

Representations of qualification, etc.

(2) No person other than a member shall hold himself or herself out as a person who is qualified to practise in Ontario as a dietitian or in a specialty of dietetics. 1991, c. 26, s. 7 (2).

Prince Edward Island

The rules that impact the practices of Holistic Nutritionists in Prince Edward Island are primarily drawn from the *Medical Act* and the *Dietitians Act*.

The *Medical Act* makes it an offence to practise or to hold oneself out as being qualified to practise Medicine unless licensed to do so under the Act. The *Medical Act* also contains an illustrative list of practice areas (e.g., surgery, obstetrics) that are deemed to be included within the meaning of "Medicine." As the definition of the practice of Medicine in the Act does not include any defined activities, the question of whether in providing services a Holistic Nutritionist is practising Medicine would be determined by the Courts, although practising Medicine is generally interpreted to include, among other things, diagnosing and treating diseases and disorders.

The *Dietitians Act* defines the scope of a registered Dietitian's practice. While it does not restrict an unregulated professional from carrying on a Dietitian's practice, it does makes it unlawful for unregulated professionals to hold themselves out as being registered Dietitians who are entitled to engage in the practice of Dietetics.

The *Dietitians Act* reserves the title "Dietitian" and several related variations for exclusive use by Registered Dietitians. It also prohibits anyone who is not a registered Dietitian from using any title, etc. that implies he or she is a registered Dietitian. As the Act does not restrict in any way the use of the title "Nutritionist," Holistic Nutritionists may use it as part of a professional title and in their advertising and marketing literature.

Naturopathy is not a Regulated Health Profession in P.E.I.

A Holistic Nutritionist who is not a member of a Regulated Health Profession in P.E.I may carry on a conventional nutritional counselling practice provided he or she: (1) does not practice Medicine as this term is defined in the *Medical Act* (see next page) and has been interpreted by the Courts; (2) does not market themselves to the public using a title reserved for registered Dietitians or any another Regulated Health Profession or otherwise falsely represent themselves as being a registered Dietitian, etc.; and (3) otherwise complies with laws of general application.

For a better understanding of how the Courts have interpreted "practice of Medicine" as well as other relevant terms, the reader should review the discussion of terminology in the next chapter.

Restrictions on Activities in Prince Edward Island

Medical Act
SNL 2005 c. M-4.01

s. 1 In this Act

(q) "practice of medicine" means the practice of medicine, surgery, obstetrics, pathology, radiology and the specialities thereof, but does not include veterinary surgery

s. 56 (1) Except as provided in this Act, and the regulations, no person, other than a medical practitioner who holds a license or a professional corporation which holds a license, shall
> (a) publicly or privately, for hire, gain or hope of reward, practise or offer to practise medicine;
> (b) hold himself or itself out in any way to be entitled to practise medicine; or
> (c) assume any title or description implying or designed to lead the public to believe that he or it is entitled to practise medicine.

(2) No person is entitled to receive a fee, reward or remuneration for professional services rendered or medicine or medical supplies supplied to any person in the practice of Medicine unless registered and licensed at the time the services were provided, or medicine or supplies were.

Restrictions on Professional Titles in Prince Edward Island

Dietitians Act
SNL2005 c. D-23.1

s. 1 In this Act

(e) "dietetics" means the professional practice of applying scientific knowledge of foods and nutrition to human health and, in particular,
> (i) assessing the nutritional status and requirements of individuals or groups of individuals,
> (ii) designing general standards and determining care plans appropriate to meet nutritional requirements,
> (iii) designing, evaluating and communicating to the public, information on nutrition matters for the purposes of health education and consumer protection,
> (iv) directing nutritional therapy,
> (v) ensuring the nutritional quality and safety of food service in a health-care institution or program;

(f) "dietitian" means a person registered under this Act

s. 20 No person other than a registered dietitian holding a valid certificate shall

    (a) engage in or carry on the practice of dietetics under the title of "dietitian", "RD", "P.Dt.", "dietetiste", "Dt.p" or such other similar designation as may be prescribed in regulations;

    (b) call herself or himself a "registered dietitian", "RD", "P.Dt.", "dietetiste professionelle", "Dt.p." or other similar designation as may be prescribed; or

    (c) take or use any name, title, or description implying or calculated to lead people to infer that the person is a registered dietitian.

Quebec

The rules that impact the practices of Holistic Nutritionists in Quebec are primarily drawn from the *Medical Act* and chapter 26 of the Quebec *Professional Code* which defines the profession of Dietetics in Quebec and establishes the "Ordre professionnel des diététistes du Québec" as the regulatory body for Dietitians.

The *Medical Act* defines the practice of Medicine and establishes a list of reserved activities (i.e., Restricted Activities) that may only be performed by members of the medical profession duly licensed under the Act. In reviewing the reserved activities, the reader will see that diagnosing illness, determining medical treatment, prescribing medications and other substances, and prescribing treatment are all reserved. In understanding the meaning of "determining medical treatment," reference must also be made back to the broad definition of the practice of Medicine included in the *Medical Act*: "The practice of Medicine consists in assessing and diagnosing any deficiency in the health of human beings and in preventing and treating illness to maintain or restore health."

Chapter 26 of the Quebec *Professional Code* defines the practice of Dietetics and identifies two procedures that may only be performed by members of the Ordre professionnel des diététistes du Québec. These procedures involve determining a nutritional plan where "an individual prescription indicates that nutrition is a determining factor in the treatment of illness" and monitoring the nutritional status of a person who is on such a plan. The use of the word "prescription," which the *Medical Act* defines to be within the exclusive purview of a medical doctor (see the *Medical Act* s 35(6) below), indicates the nutritional plan must be prescribed by a medical doctor as part of the treatment of a diseases to become a reserved act (i.e., Restricted Activity) of members of the Ordre professionnel des diététistes du Quebec.

Chapter 26 of the Quebec *Professional Code* also reserves several titles for exclusive use by members of the Ordre professionnel des dietetistes du Québec, including "Dietitian" and "Nutritionist," several related abbreviations, and any other title that may wrongfully imply a person is a member of the Order.

Naturopathy is not a Regulated Health Profession in Quebec.

A Holistic Nutritionist who is not a member of a Regulated Health Profession in Quebec may carry on a conventional nutritional counselling practice provided he or she: (1) does not perform any reserved activities (i.e., Restricted Activities); (2) does not market themselves to the public using a title reserved for members of the Ordre professionnel des diététistes du Québec or

Medical Doctors or any another Regulated Health Profession; and (3) otherwise complies with laws of general application.

Quebec establishes reserved activities on a profession by profession basis. I have summarized activities that are reserved for Medical practitioners and Dietitians. The *Professional Code* provisions for other Regulated Health Professions should be consulted if your practice includes activities other than providing general nutritional counselling to promote health and wellness, or if you provide any other services that you suspect may be an activity commonly practised by another Regulated Health Profession in Quebec.

For a better understanding of how terms such as "diagnose" and "treat" are to be interpreted, the reader should review the discussion of terminology in the following chapter.

Restrictions on Activities in Quebec

Medical Act
R.S.Q., chapter M-9

s. 31. The practice of medicine consists in assessing and diagnosing any deficiency in the health of human beings and in preventing and treating illness to maintain or restore health.

Reserved activities.

The following activities in the practice of medicine are reserved to physicians:

(1) diagnosing illnesses;

(2) prescribing diagnostic examinations;

(3) using diagnostic techniques that are invasive or entail risks of injury;

(4) determining medical treatment;

(5) prescribing medications and other substances;

(6) prescribing treatment;

(7) using techniques or applying treatments that are invasive or entail risks of injury, including aesthetic procedures;

(8) providing clinical monitoring of the condition of patients whose state of health is problematic;

(9) providing pregnancy care and conducting deliveries; and

(10) making decisions as to the use of restraint measures.

DIVISION VII
ILLEGAL PRACTICE OF MEDICINE

Acts restricted to physicians.

s. 43. Subject to the rights and privileges expressly granted by law to other professionals, no person may engage in any activity described in the second paragraph of section 31, unless he is a physician.

Professional Code
C-26,

s. 37 Every member of one of the following professional orders may engage in the following professional acidities in addition to those otherwise allowed him by law:

(c) the Ordre professionnel des dietetistes du Quebec: assess the nutritional status of a person and determine and ensure the implementation of a response strategy designed to tailor diet to needs in order to maintain or restore health.

s. 37.1 Every member of one of the following professional orders may engage in the following professional activities, which are reserved to such members with the scope of the activities they may engage under section 37

(1) the Ordre professionnel des diététistes du Québec:

   (a) Determine a nutritional plan, including the appropriate feeding route, where an individual prescription indicates that nutrition is a determining factor in the treatment of illness; and

   (b) Monitor the nutritional status of persons whose nutritional treatment plan has been determined

s. 37.2 A person shall not in any manner engage in a professional activity reserved under section s. 37.1 to members of a professional order, claim to have the right to do so or act in such a way as to lead to the belief that the person is authorized to do so, unless the person holds a valid, appropriate permit and is entered on the roll of the order empowered to issue the permit except if it is allowed by law.

s. 38 Nothing in this division shall be interpreted as giving to members of an order to which it applies the exclusive right to engage in the activities described in section 37, in letters patent constituting such order or in an amalgamation or integration order.

Restrictions on Professional Titles in Quebec

Professional Code
C-26,

s. 36 No person shall in any way whatsoever;

(c) use the title "Dieician", "Dietitian" or "Nutritionist" or any other title or abbreviation which may lead to the belief that his is a dietician, a dietitian or a nutritionist, or use initials which may lead to the belief that he is a dietician, dietitian or a nutritionist, or the initials "P.Dt.", "Dt.P" or "R.D." unless he holds a valid permit for that purpose and is entered on the roll of the Ordre professionnel des dietetistes du Quebec.

s. 37.2 A person shall not in any manner engage in a professional activity reserved under section 37.1 to members of a professional order, claim to have the right to do so or act in such a way as to lead to the belief that the person is authorized to do so, unless the person holds a valid, appropriate permit and is entered on the roll of the order empowered to issue the permit except if it is allowed by law.

Saskatchewan

The rules that impact the practices of Holistic Nutritionists in Saskatchewan are primarily drawn from the *Medical Profession Act*, the *Naturopathic Act* and the *Dietitians Act*.

The *Medical Profession Act* makes it an offence for anyone who is not a member of the College of Physicians and Surgeons of Saskatchewan to, among other things, engage in or profess to engage in any aspect of the practice of Medicine, or to furnish any medicine or treat any disease or ailment by medicine for hire, gain or hope of reward. As "practice of Medicine" is not defined by the statute, the question of whether in providing services a Holistic Nutritionist is practising Medicine would be determined by the Courts, although it generally includes, among other things, diagnosing and treating diseases and disorders.

The *Medical Profession Act* also restricts persons who are not members of the medical profession from using titles such as "Doctor" and "Surgeon" or any other name or title that wrongfully infers a person is registered to practice Medicine.

The *Naturopathic Act* makes it an offence to practice naturopathy or use the title "Naturopath," etc. unless authorized to do so under the Act. This Act also defines the practice of Naturopathy to be "the art of healing by natural methods as taught in recognized schools of naturopathy." While the "art of healing" is not defined in the statute, common sense implies it means, at a minimum, diagnosing and treating diseases and disorders

The main problem with this definition is that one must look to the curriculum of Naturopathic schools to know what activities are exclusively reserved for Naturopaths, and these curriculums may be inconsistent or even conflict. The Canadian College of Naturopathic Medicine[18] defines Naturopathic Medicine as "a distinct system of primary health care that addresses the root causes of illness, and promotes health and healing using natural therapies. It supports your body's own healing ability using an integrated approach to disease diagnosis, treatment and prevention that includes [ed. among modalities] . . . clinical nutrition."

As Naturopathic Medicine extends beyond merely treating diseases to include promoting health through nutrition, there is some question in Saskatchewan whether the conventional practice of a Holistic Nutritionist falls within the scope of a Naturopath's practice and is therefore prohibited by the *Naturopathic Act*, or whether use of the phrase "art of healing" in the statute means only to the extent Holistic Nutrition is used to treat diseases and disorders, leaving open the right for Holistic Nutritionists to "promote health."

---

[18] Canadian College of Naturopathic Medicine [online]. [Accessed February 15, 2011.] <http://www.ccnm.edu>.

It may be of some comfort to Holistic Nutritionists to know that the Supreme Court of Canada has determined that statutes that create professional monopolies are to be strictly construed "so that anything which is not clearly prohibited to non-members of the profession may be done by them."[19] It could be argued that this interpretive guideline tips the scales in favour of Holistic Nutritionists.

The *Dietitians Act* does not define the practice of Dietetics nor restrict in any way who may carry on a nutritional consulting practice. The Act reserves the title "Dietitian" and several related variations for exclusive use by registered Dietitians. It also prohibits anyone who is not a registered Dietitian from using any title, etc. that implies he or she is a registered Dietitian. As the Act does not restrict in any way the use of the title "Nutritionist," Holistic Nutritionists may use it as part of a professional title and in their marketing and advertising.

As noted above, an argument can be made that the practice of a Holistic Nutritionist in Saskatchewan falls within the exclusive practice scope of registered Naturopaths. Unfortunately, I was unable to locate any reported Court decisions directly reviewing this question. Subject to this qualification, a Holistic Nutritionist who is not a member of a Regulated Health Profession in Saskatchewan may carry on a conventional nutritional practice provided he or she: (1) does not practice Medicine as this term is defined in the *Medical Act* and has been interpreted by the Courts, or otherwise furnish medicine or treat any disease, etc. by medicine for a fee; (2) does not practice Naturopathy as this term is defined in the *Naturopathic Act*; (3) does not market themselves to the public using a title reserved for registered Dietitians, Medical Doctors or registered Naturopaths or any another Regulated Health Profession or otherwise falsely represent themselves as being a registered Dietitian, Medical Doctor, Naturopath, etc. and (4) otherwise complies with laws of general application.

For a better understanding of how terms such as "practice of Medicine," etc. are to be interpreted, the reader should review the discussion of terminology in next chapter.

Restrictions on Activities in Saskatchewan

The Medical Profession Act
1981c. M-10.1 of the Statutes of Saskatchewan, 1980-81

Interpretation

s. 2 In this Act

(k) "practice" means the practice of medicine, surgery or midwifery

---

[19] R. v. Windrum. See also Laporte v. Collège des Pharmaciens (Québec) (1974), 23 C.C.C. (2d) 45.

s. 80(1) A person who is not registered under this Act and who:

    (a) for hire, gain or hope of reward:

        (i) engages in, professes to engage in or advertises to give advice in any aspect of practice; or

        (ii) furnishes any medicine or treats any disease or ailment by medicine, drugs or any Form of treatment, influence or appliance;

    (b) takes or uses any name, title, addition or description representing, implying or calculated to lead people to infer that he is registered under this Act to practise, or that he is recognized by law as a physician, surgeon or podiatric surgeon;

    (c) assumes, uses or employs the term "doctor", "surgeon", "physician" or "podiatric surgeon" or any affix or prefix indicative of any such title as an occupational designation that relates to the treatment of human ailments, or advertises or holds himself out as such;

    (d) pretends to be a physician, doctor of medicine, surgeon, podiatric surgeon, practitioner or healer of the sick; or

    (e) assumes any title, addition or description other than that which he actually possesses and is legally entitled to use under this Act;

is guilty of an offence and liable on summary conviction, in the case of a first offence, to a fine of not more than $5,000, in the case of a second offence, to a fine of not more than $10,000, and, in the case of a third or subsequent offence, to a fine of not more than $15,000.

The Naturopathy Act

Being Chapter N-4 of The Revised Statutes of Saskatchewan, 1978 (effective February 26, 1979) as amended by the Statutes of Saskatchewan, 1980-81, c.21 and 62; 1984-85-86, c.16; 1989-90, c.54 and 1994, c.P-37.1; 2004, c.L-16.1; and 2010, c.B-12 and c.19.

s. 2 In this Act:

(d) "naturopathic practitioner" means a person who is registered as such under this Act;

(e) "naturopathy" means the art of healing by natural methods as taught in recognized schools of naturopathy.

s. 9 No person, other than a naturopathic practitioner registered under this Act as a member of the association shall engage in the practice of naturopathy or use the title "Naturopathic Practitioner", "Naturopath", "Doctor of Naturopathy" or any word, title or designation, abbreviated or otherwise, to imply that he is engaged in the practice of naturopathy, and every person who contravenes this section is guilty of an offence against this Ac Prohibition against unauthorized practice

s. 11(1) Every person who practises naturopathy, either alone or in conjunction with any other method of treatment of the human body for disease and the causes of disease, for hire, gain, reward or remuneration, or the hope or expectation thereof, unless he is duly registered to practise as a naturopath under this Act is guilty of an offence against this Act.

(2) Every person who, not being registered as a naturopathic practitioner under this Act, or who, having been so registered and whose registration has been cancelled or is under suspension, practises or holds himself out as practising naturopathy, either alone or in conjunction with any other method of treatment of the human body for disease and the causes of disease, or advertises or uses any prefix or suffix to his name signifying that he is qualified to practise naturopathy either alone or in conjunction with any other method of treatment of the human body for disease and the causes of disease, is guilty of an offence against this Act.

Restrictions on Professional Titles in Saskatchewan

The Dietitians Act
c. D-27.1 of the Statutes of Saskatchewan, 2001

Protection of title

s. 21 No person other than a member shall use the title "Dietitian", "Registered Dietitian" or "Professional Dietitian" or the abbreviation "R.D." or "P.Dt." or any word, title or designation, abbreviated or otherwise, to imply that the person is a member.

Chapter 4
Interpreting Key Terms

In the previous chapter I reviewed the rules that most directly restrict the right of a Holistic Nutritionist to carry on a conventional nutritional consulting practice in the various Canadian provinces. To more fully understand the scope of the law, however, it is also necessary to look at the meanings of the key words and phrases used in these rules. For example, while it is useful to know that Holistic Nutritionists in the provinces of Manitoba[20], New Brunswick, Newfoundland and Labrador, Nova Scotia, Prince Edward Island and Saskatchewan can generally provide nutritional counselling services provided they do not engage in the "practice of Medicine," this information is far more useful if we also understand what activities are included within "the practice of Medicine." The same goes for other terms, such as "diagnosis," "treatment," "diseases," etc. that are used throughout the laws of the different provinces.

Sometimes words and phrases are defined within the statute relying on their use. When this is the case, the statute can be understood with the highest degree of certainty. For example, the Nova Scotia *Medical Act* defines the practice of Medicine to include the activities of diagnosing and treating diseases. So in this province, we know with absolute certainty that the "practice of Medicine" includes these activities.

When a statute does not provide this guidance, one must search to see how the words and phrases have been interpreted by judges over the years, or in legal dictionaries, and even in similar legislation of other provinces and countries. The answers provided by this research can be a good indicator of how a Court may proceed but cannot be determinative. Courts can and do interpret the same words and phrases in different ways, sometimes even reaching quite conflicting decisions. This can happen for many reasons, including the personalities of the judges involved

---

[20] Manitoba is currently in the process of changing how it regulates Health Professions. An overview of the changes it is implementing can be found in Chapter 3.

and the different facts that exist in the cases before them. In one set of facts, their sense of justice may direct them towards interpreting a word or phrase broadly, in another, narrowly. As troublesome as this uncertainty is for Holistic Nutritionists, it is a fact of life.

This point was well illustrated in the Sandhar case, which I first mentioned in Chapter 2. The reader may recall this case involved a Homeopath in Alberta who prescribed a liver cleanser as treatment for an inflamed liver, which he diagnosed using a machine that measured the flow of energy of various organs from acqua pressure meridian points. I believe it is safe to say this was not a diagnostic procedure, diagnosis or treatment likely to have been followed by a conventional medical doctor operating in Alberta at that time. Perhaps it is for this reason that the trial judge found Mr. Sandhar not guilty of practising Medicine. The judges on appeal, however, took a different view and found Mr. Sandhar guilty.

The facts of a case have a very important impact on the result. In the words of former Chief Justice Moss, of the Ontario Court of Appeal[21] while considering whether the phrase "practice of Medicine" means an attempt to cure or alleviate disease by the use of drugs:

> But unless there is a concrete case with the facts proved or known, how is it possible to say whether or not the words of sec. 49 are applicable? If the answer given was that if it were shewn [sic] that a person not registered under the Ontario *Medical Act* attempted to cure or alleviate disease by methods and course of treatment known to medical science and adopted and used in their practice by medical practitioners registered under the Act, or advised or prescribed treatment for disease or illness such as would be advised or prescribed by the registered practitioner, then, although what was done, prescribed or administered did not involve the use or application of any drug or other substance having or supposed to have the property of curing or alleviating disease, he might be held to be practising medicine with the meaning of section 49, it would still leave the matter to be dealt with in a concrete case, in which the ultimate decision must turn upon the facts found.

So with this bit of guidance in mind, let's see how some key words and phrases have been defined by the Courts and in the legal literature to gain a better idea of how they may be interpreted and applied in the future.

Diagnosis

Within all Canadian provinces, with the exception of Alberta, the right to lawfully make a diagnosis is restricted to one or more Regulated Health Professions. It very important to

---

[21] Ontario Medical Act, Re (1906) 13 O.L.R. 501

understand, therefore, what making a diagnosis means. Here are some of the ways this term has been defined:

> The identification of a disease by means of a patient's symptoms.[22]
>
> To determine the nature of the disease or disorder in a given case.[23]
>
> The determination of what kind of disease a patient is suffering from, especially the art of distinguishing between several possibilities. Also, the verdict (the name of the disease) decided upon.[24]

The Sandhar decision, referred to previously, also provides instruction about what it means to make a diagnosis. In this case, a Homeopath was found to have made a diagnosis even though he used an energy test to identify liver and lung inflammation resulting from a buildup of toxins. This decision illustrates the point that someone can be found to have provided a diagnosis even if they used diagnostic procedures that are outside the normal practice of conventional Medicine. What matters is not the procedures used, but rather the results achieved—the determination or identification of a disease or disorder the patient is suffering from. Here is a quote from the decision:

> The Respondent [ed. Sandhar] examined Miss Lewis and stated to her that she had lung congestion and liver and kidney inflammation. That act, on his part, fits directly within s. 77(1) (a) in that he stated an ability or willingness to diagnose a human disease or illness. Dr. LeRiche gave evidence that these two complaints were in fact illness.

The term "diagnosis" is very broadly defined and is not connected to any particular process or health modality. Instead, it hinges on the rendering of a conclusion or verdict that an individual is suffering from a disease, disorder, etc.

Diseases & Disorders

Legislation that regulates the act of making a diagnosis links it to making a diagnosis of a disease or disorder. Once again, you will see these terms are broadly defined and can logically be interpreted to include virtually any deviation from what is considered to be the healthy norm, including resulting from nutritional deficiencies.

> Disease – An unhealthy condition of the body (or part of it) or the mind; illness, sickness[25]

---

[22] R. v. Windrum
[23] J. E. Schmidt, *Attorney's Dictionary of Medicine* (New York: Mathew Bender and Company, Inc., 2005)
[24] Ibid.

Disease – 1. Morbus; illness; sickness; an interruption, cessation or disorder of bodily functions, systems, or organs. 2. A morbid entity characterized by at least two of these criteria, recognized etiologic agent(s) identifiable group of signs and symptoms or consistent anatomical alterations.[26]

Disorder – A condition marked by deviation from normal activity or function; a disease; an abnormal mental or physical condition.[27]

Disorder – A disturbance of function, structure or both resulting from a genetic or embryonic failure in development or from exogenous factors such as poison, trauma or disease.[28]

Drug

Several provinces define the practice of Medicine to include prescribing drugs, or expressly restrict this activity to members of specified Regulated Health Professions. In the other provinces it is reasonable to assume prescribing drugs is activity that would typically found to be within the scope of the practice of Medicine. Knowing when a substance is a "drug" then, is very important. Unfortunately, the rules in many provinces do not define what a drug is, for the purposes of this restriction. Where the rules do (e.g., in Ontario and Alberta), it is typically defined to be a restricted (prescription) drug or controlled medication. If the reader practises in a province that does define a drug for this purpose, the rules should be consulted.

Where rules do not define what a drug is, other sources must be consulted to determine the types of substances a Court may conclude are drugs. In Canada, a logical starting place for making this determination is the federal *Food and Drugs Act*[29], which applies to the manufacturing, promotion and sale of all foods and drugs in Canada. The *Food and Drugs Act* defines a drug as follows:

"drug" includes any substance or mixture of substances manufactured, sold or represented for use in:

(a) the diagnosis, treatment, mitigation or prevention of a disease, disorder or abnormal physical state, or its symptoms, in human beings or animals,

(b) restoring, correcting or modifying organic functions in human beings or animals, or

---

[25] R v. Windrum.
[26] William R. Hensyl, ed., *Stedman's Medical Dictionary*, 25th ed. (Baltimore: Williams & Wilkins, 1990).
[27] J. E. Schmidt, *Attorney's Dictionary of Medicine* (New York: Mathew Bender and Company, Inc., 2005).
[28] William R. Hensyl, ed., *Stedman's Medical Dictionary*, 25th ed. (Baltimore: Williams & Wilkins, 1990).
[29] *Food and Drugs Act*, R.S., 1985, c. F-27

(c) disinfection in premises in which food is manufactured, prepared or kept;

By contrast it defines food to be:

> "food" includes any article manufactured, sold or represented for use as food or drink for human beings, chewing gum, and any ingredient that may be mixed with food for any purpose whatever;

The frustrating thing about this Act is that all products that are consumed must be classified under these one of these two categories—and the determination of which category a substance falls into depends not upon what the substance is (e.g., a man-made chemical or agent) but rather what is said or represented about it. For Holistic Nutritionists trying to understand what they can and cannot recommend, this obviously creates a problem. In any province where a "drug" is not otherwise defined, it is very logical to assume the definition contained in the federal *Food and Drugs Act* should apply and this definition clearly states that any substance, even one that is normally viewed to be a food, becomes a drug when preventive or curative claims are made about it.[30] Does this mean a Holistic Nutritionist who makes such a claim about a food is in fact prescribing a drug and therefore practising Medicine or engaging in a Restricted Activity?

I don't believe any reasonable person would seriously argue this is what our legislators intended when they saw fit to restrict who may prescribe drugs. Unfortunately, as I was unable to locate any Court decisions expressly dealing with this question, this conclusion cannot be ruled out. Notwithstanding, I believe if one moves beyond the bare language of the *Foods and Drugs Act* a more reasoned argument can be developed that supports the conclusion that a Holistic Nutritionist who makes health claims about foods and nutritional supplements in the course of a professional nutritional counselling practice should not be seen to be prescribing drugs and thereby crossing the threshold into the practice of Medicine, or a Restricted Activity.

First, I believe in those provinces where "drug" is not defined, rather than looking exclusively to the *Food and Drugs Act*, it is better to look to the rules of other provinces where the term "drug" is defined, because definitions should be considered within the context of the rules in which they are used. The *Food and Drugs Act* exists to protect consumers from fraudulent product claims and to ensure the safety of the products we consume. This is different than the purpose of a Medical Act, or a Regulated Health Professions Act, which exists to ensure only individuals with the requisite training can do certain things, such as prescribe drugs. So what federal Parliament

---

[30] In Wrigley Canada v. R. (2000) 96 A.C.W.S. (3d) 888 the Federal Court of Appeal confirmed that under the *Food and Drugs Act* a substance may be classified as both a food and a drug at the same time, depending upon the representations made about it. As a result, chewing gum, which is expressly identified as food in the Act, was also seen to be a drug, when the manufacturer sought to include on the product label for its sugarless "Extra" gum a claim that the gum "prevents Tooth Decay."

may want to call a "drug" for the purpose of controlling manufacturing, labelling and advertising, a provincial legislature may not want to regard as a "drug" for the purposes of controlling who may "prescribe" it. The definition of drugs in the *Food and Drugs Act*, for example, includes many over-the-counter products anyone of any age is free to purchase.

In provinces where the Regulated Health Profession legislation does define the word "drug," such as Alberta and Ontario, it consistently means a substance that is controlled—such as prescription medication, and narcotics, and not substances that are historically viewed to be foods, or over-the-counter supplements that are available without restriction.

Second, even if one looks at the definitions contained in the *Food and Drugs Act*, one really must consider how the words "food" and "drug" are interpreted and applied by Health Canada, and not just to the plain language of the Act. The definitions in the *Food and Drugs Act* were drafted very broadly to give Health Canada a fair amount of flexibility when classifying consumable products. So much turns upon Health Canada's exercise of its discretion.

In response to the huge growth in the market for natural health products over the last twenty or so years, Health Canada developed a new regulation known as the *Natural Health Products Regulation*. The purpose of this regulation is to create an appropriate regulatory regime for natural substances that are marketed and sold for their curative or preventive properties. This regulation defines a Natural Health Product to be:

> "a substance set out in Schedule 1 [ed. – essentially, a plant or plant material, an alga, a bacterium, a fungus or a non-human animal material] or a combination of substances in which all the medicinal ingredients are substances set out in Schedule 1, a homeopathic medicine or a traditional medicine, that is manufactured, sold or represented for use in
>
> (a) the diagnosis, treatment, mitigation or prevention of a disease, disorder or abnormal physical state or its symptoms in humans;
>
> (b) restoring or correcting organic functions in humans; or
>
> (c) modifying organic functions in humans, such as modifying those functions in a manner that maintains or promotes health."

As a result of this regulation, Natural Health Products while technically "drugs" under the *Food and Drugs Act*, are regulated by Health Canada as a different subset of product altogether:

> In developing the *Natural Health Products Regulations*, Health Canada's intent was to cover products that consumers can select and use themselves, without the need to consult a health care provider and obtain a prescription. Accordingly, with the exception of homeopathic medicines, products with ingredients that are required to be sold pursuant to

a prescription (listed in Schedule F to the *Food and Drug Regulations*) are not natural health products.[31]

Health Canada also offers guidance for understanding the definition of "food." In a recent document[32], Health Canada looked at the differences between food and Natural Health Products (i.e., natural substances that are promoted for their curative or preventive properties and which would otherwise be regulated as drugs). In this guidance document, Health Canada made the following comments about how it decides whether something is a food or a Natural Health Product:

1. **Composition** – When a food or ingredient is present in a product solely to provide nourishment, nutrition or hydration, or to satisfy hunger, thirst or a desire for taste, texture or flavour this is an indication that the product is a food. A product that is or that contains an added ingredient that has no known food purpose but that has only a therapeutic use is likely to be classified a Natural Health Product.

2. **Representations** – Claims that speak to a product having therapeutic uses that are not based on the use of the product as a food suggest the product is a Natural Health Product.

3. **Format** – Natural Health Products are typically sold in a format that allows them to be consumed in measured or controlled amounts (doses). If a product is sold in a particular food format (e.g., a beverage) that lends itself to dosing (e.g., sold in single dosage units or it is sold with a measure that indicates it to be consumed in controlled amounts) this is one indication that the product is a Natural Health Product

4. **Public Perception and History** – If a product has a historical pattern of use as a food or if the public perception associated with the use of a product in the marketplace is that it is a food, these are indications that the product is a food rather than a Natural Health Product. Conversely, if the public perception associated with a product and its history and pattern of use indicate it is sold for a therapeutic purpose this supports the conclusion that the product is a Natural Health Product.

---

[31] Health Canada, *Overview of the Natural Health Products Regulations Guidance Document* [online], <http://www.hc-sc.gc.ca/dhp-mps/prodnatur/legislation/docs/regula-regle_over-apercu-eng.php#21>.

[32] Health Canada, *Classification of Products at the Food – Natural Health Product Interface: Products in Food Formats* [online], Natural Health Products Directorate, Food Directorate, March 2009. <http://www.hc-sc.gc.ca/dhp-mps/prodnatur/legislation/docs/food-nhp-aliments-psn-guide-eng.php>.

For Holistic Nutritionists whose provinces directly or indirectly restrict but do not define what it means to prescribe "drugs," there are several factors to be taken into account when recommending foods and supplements for clients. First, if we look to other provinces where "drug" is defined for guidance, we find it tends to mean substances that are controlled—such as prescription medication, and narcotics. Second, if we look to Canada's *Food and Drugs Act* for guidance, we find that Natural Health Products inhabit a special regulatory world where they are treated as neither foods nor drugs. While I cannot say for certain that no Court would ever find a Holistic Nutritionist to have prescribed a drug when recommending a food or Natural Health Product to clients, I do believe it is unlikely, because a strong argument can be advanced that these substances are not and should not be viewed to be drugs in the context of Regulated Health Profession legislation.

Practice of Medicine

The provinces of British Columbia, Manitoba, New Brunswick, Nova Scotia, Prince Edward Island, Newfoundland and Labrador, and Saskatchewan currently prohibit unauthorized persons from engaging in the practice of Medicine. Of these provinces, four—British Columbia, Manitoba, Nova Scotia and Saskatchewan—also deem the practice of Medicine to include diagnosing and treating diseases and disorders and other specific activities.

If the province in which you practise restricts the practice of Medicine, you should review the rules to determine whether any specific activities are restricted. You should also be aware that these lists are not typically exhaustive. By this I mean in all cases other than British Columbia the rules also leave it open for the Courts to decide other procedures and activities constitute the practice of Medicine.

So, in addition to any specific procedures identified within the rules as being included with the practice of Medicine, what other activities should be avoided?

If you practise in one of the provinces referred to above, I believe the safest approach is to avoid engaging in any activities other provinces have deemed to be Restricted Activities, or included within their definition of "practice of Medicine." The reader can develop a complete list of these activities and procedures by reviewing the legislation summaries for the provinces set out in Chapter 3. I have also set out below an edited list that includes the activities and procedures I believe Holistic Nutritionists should be particularly aware of because they either involve an aspect of nutritional counselling or are activities an unaware Holistic Nutritionist could engage in while trying to help a client.

1. Advertising, holding out to the public or representing in any manner that one is authorized to practise medicine.

2. Offering or undertaking to prescribe, order, give or administer any drug or medicine for the use of any other person.

3. Offering or undertaking to prevent or to diagnose, correct or treat in any manner or by any means, methods, devices or instrumentalities any disease, illness, pain, wound, fracture, infirmity, defect or abnormal physical or mental condition of any person.

4. Offering or undertaking to perform any obstetrical procedure or surgical operation upon any person.

5. Ordering or receiving reports of screening or diagnostic tests.

6. Performing a procedure on tissue below the skin, etc.

7. Inserting or removing an instrument or a device, hand or finger into a body opening.

8. Administering a substance by injection, inhalation, etc.

9. Prescribing, compounding or dispensing or administering a drug or vaccine.

10. In relation to a therapeutic diet that is administered by enteral instillation or parenteral instillation:
    a. selecting ingredients for the diet; or
    b. compounding or administering the diet.

11. Administering a high velocity, low amplitude thrust to move a joint of the spine within its anatomical range of motion.

12. Performing a psycho-social intervention with an expectation of modifying a substantial disorder of thought, mood, perception, orientation or memory that grossly impairs judgment, behaviour, the capacity to recognize reality, or the ability to meet the ordinary demands of life.

13. Allergy challenge testing or allergy desensitizing treatment involving injection, scratch tests or inhalation, and allergy challenge testing by any means with respect to a patient who has had a previous anaphylactic reaction.

Over the years, various Courts in Canada have also opined on the activities that may or may not constitute the practice of Medicine. I have summarized below key points identified in some of these decisions along with brief quotations from the judges to help the reader get a better feel for how the Courts look at the practice of Medicine.

- There can be no definitive definition of Medicine:

    Nevertheless, we cannot say that the profession, wide as have been its conquests and extended the scope of its practice, has taken all knowledge of the art of healing for its province, and therefore the question submitted (in its alternative form) does not admit of a universal answer in the affirmative. We can only say that the words to practise medicine may include cases in which the remedy prescribed, etc., does not involve the use of drugs or other substances. Every case must stand and be determined upon its own facts and circumstances. We cannot lay down a rule or formulate an answer which will include all.[33]

- The practice of Medicine is broader than merely prescribing drugs and medication:

    'Practising medicine' is not a definite and finally established term. There is much room for argument both as to what should be called 'medicine' and as to what should be called 'practising'. . . . The term 'practising medicine' need not and does not, in my opinion, necessarily involve only the prescribing or administering of a drug or other medicinal substance, but may well include all such means and methods of treatment or prevention of disease as are from time to time generally taught in the medical colleges and practised by the regular or registered practitioner. . . .[34]

- The practice of Medicine involves monetary gain:

    A person in order to render himself liable for practising medicine under the *Medical Act* [R.S.O. 1897, c. 176, s. 49], must have, for gain, prescribed or recommended for trial a particular remedy selected by himself as appropriate to the symptoms described by the patient.[35]

- Where a client selects two alternative remedies stating an opinion as to which one is believed to be the better of the two does not necessarily constitute the practice of Medicine:

    If the patient selects a remedy for himself, making up his own mind as to what he ought to take, there is no offence. A druggist is allowed, it appears, to state fully the qualities and properties of two or more remedies, and even to say which in his opinion is the better

---

[33] Ontario Medical Act, Re (1906) 13 O.L.R. 501
[34] Ibid.
[35] R. v. Coulson as cited in R. v. Valleau, (1900) 3 C.C.C. 435

remedy or compound, but he must stop short of recommending which remedy the patient had better take for his alleged trouble or complaint.[36]

- The practice of Medicine involves more than an isolated activity:

  The single act of prescribing medicine to one person on one day will not amount to a practising of medicine . . . Evidence of acts of practising antecedent . . . and possibly . . . subsequent to the date laid in the conviction . . . might be given . . . as establishing . . . a practising of medicine. These acts, however, must be sufficiently approximate in point of time to afford evidence of practising, rather than tending to establish the commission of a separate offence.[37]

  The words of the Act appear to me to point rather to an habitual, or at all events a continuous course of conduct, that to an isolated act as constituting the offence.[38]

- An isolated act may be sufficient for a practice, if there is also the intention to carry on a business:

  It was stated in the judgment of this Division in Rex v. Cruikshanks (1914) 6 W.W.R. 524, at 526, 7 Alta. L.R. 92, at 96, 23 C.C.C. 23, that: "There is no doubt that the law does not contemplate a single act as constituting the practice of a profession or trade," but it was also pointed out by Beck, J., in Rex v. Stimmel, [1923] 3 W.W.R. 1185, at 1201, 19 Alta. L.R. 719, at 738, that "a single or isolated act coupled with an intent to carry on business would suffice."[39]

- Practising a health modality that is wholly outside conventional Medicine is not the practice of Medicine:

  Insofar as the evidence discloses it [ed. Acupuncture] is not recognized by the Alberta College of Physicians and Surgeons as a branch of 'medicine', nor is it taught as an approved course of medical education at any university in North America. . . On the bases of all of the foregoing, I am not satisfied beyond a reasonable doubt that the accused in this case may be convicted of the charge as laid. I am satisfied that his conduct was not in contravention of the particular wording of s. 64 nor was it in contravention of the spirit and intent of the Alberta Medical Profession Act.[40]

---

[36] Ibid.
[37] R. v. Lee (1901) 3 C.C.C. 435
[38] Apothecaries Co. v. Jones (1893) 1 Q.B. 89
[39] R. v. Burton, (1939) 2 D.L.R. 526
[40] R. v. Wong [1979] 6 W.W.R. 163

- Notifying a client that one is not a doctor is not determinative. It is what is done that matters.

> Windrum argued that his acts were either not intended or not perceived as practising medicine. In my view that is not relevant. The issue before the Court is whether he was practising medicine. In other words, was he diagnosing or treating patients. The learned trial judge concluded that Windrum was practising medicine and in my view there was overwhelming evidence to support that finding.[41]

If the province in which you practise restricts the practice of Medicine, the definitions for Diagnosis, Diseases & Disorders, Drugs, and Treatment should also be reviewed, as these are all aspects of practising Medicine.

Treatment

The meaning of what it is to "treat" a disease or disorder is important both in provinces where the practice of Medicine is restricted (as the act of treating a disease is commonly interpreted to be an aspect of practising Medicine) as well as in provinces in which the act of administering a treatment is a Restricted Activity. Here are some of the ways "treatment" has been defined:

> The medical or surgical management of a patient.[42]

> To manage a disease by medicinal, surgical or other measures; to care for a patient medically or surgically.[43]

> The action or management of treating a patient medically or surgically. The management and care of a patient for the purpose of combating disease or disorder.[44]

The Sandhar decision was previously reviewed in connection with the meaning of "diagnoses." But in this case, Mr. Sandhar was also found guilty of prescribing a treatment by virtue of recommending a liver cleanser to address the liver inflammation he diagnosed. As with the diagnosis, it is very unlikely a doctor practising in Alberta at the time would have prescribed the same treatment as Mr. Sandhar; however, this fact did not impact the decision. What mattered to the Court was whether the substance was intended to prevent or alleviate a disease or disorder:

> The Respondent is also in contravention of s. 76 in that pursuant to the definition in practising medicine in s. 77 of the Act, he prescribed or administered a treatment for the

---

[41] R v. Windrum
[42] William R. Hensyl, ed., *Stedman's Medical Dictionary,* 25th ed. (Baltimore: Williams & Wilkins, 1990).
[43] Ibid.
[44] Ibid.

prevention, alleviation or cure of any human disease or ailment. In particular, the Respondent sold to Miss Lewis for the sum of $10.00 a liver cleanser which was to alleviate or eliminate the problem she had with liver inflammation.[45]

This point was made even more clearly in the R. v. Kish decision involving two phytologists who prescribed hydrogen peroxide as a cure for lung cancer:

> Counsel for the accused argued that the Crown had failed to call any expert evidence to the effect that what the Kishes were doing fell within the purview of medical practice as understood by practising physicians in the Province of Alberta. In fact, it is argued by counsel for the accused that because Dr. Hoy testified for the Crown that the type of treatments being prescribed by the Kishes were not recognized by the medical profession, that this type of activity therefore fell outside of the bounds of ss. 76 and 77 of the Medical Profession Act. . . . With respect I disagree and find that regardless of the philosophical view one takes of the Medical Profession Act, the evidence of Dr. Hoy was clearly to the effect that the treatment of cancer fell squarely within his purview and other duly qualified members of the medical profession.[46]

Finally, the decision in R v.Windrum showed prescribing vitamins as a treatment still constitutes prescribing a medical treatment:

> Dr. Loewen, who was qualified as an expert, said that the diagnosis is a conclusion about the patient's condition based on her history, physical examination and tests if necessary. He went on to state that one can diagnose by examining the patient's blood. Furthermore, many of the conditions found by Windrum could be diagnosed by following the above process. In Dr. Loewen's opinion it was common practice to treat patients by prescribing vitamins or iron supplements.[47]

Once again, as with other definitions, one can see that the term "treatment" is broadly interpreted and is not restricted to a particular process or modality. When trying to decide whether one's actions constitute prescribing or administering a treatment, the key issue to focus upon is whether one is attempting to manage a disease or disorder that is recognized by Medicine, not whether the treatment itself is recognized by Medicine.[48]

---

[45] R. v. Sandhar
[46] R. v. Kish
[47] R v.Windrum
[48] Astute readers may notice that this appears to be in contradiction to the decision in R. v. Wong which was cited in the discussion of 'practice of Medicine' as standing for proposition that a health modality that is wholly outside conventional Medicine (in Wong's case acupuncture) is not the practice of Medicine. This conflict reinforces the point that it is extremely risky to try to predict in the abstract how a court will decide a particular issue. At the end

Nor is the question of prescribing treatment linked to the safety of the remedy prescribed. To return to examples I have used elsewhere in this book, scurvy is an illness and dehydration is a disorder. Prescribing vitamin C to remedy scurvy and water to remedy dehydration, while seemingly harmless prescriptions, constitutes prescribing treatment. It does not matter that the remedies are safe and widely consumed; what matters is that in making the recommendation one is attempting to manage a disease or disorder.

Finally, when considering the restrictions that relate to recommending a treatment, one must look at a prohibition that exists in *Food and Drugs Act* and that applies within all provinces, even where it is otherwise lawful for Holistic Nutritionists to prescribe treatments.

Section 3 of the *Food and Drugs Act* provides:

> 3. (1) No person shall advertise any food, drug, cosmetic or device to the general public as a treatment, preventative or cure for any of the diseases, disorders or abnormal physical states referred to in Schedule A.
>
> (2) No person shall sell any food, drug, cosmetic or device
>
> (a) that is represented by label, or
>
> (b) that the person advertises to the general public
>
> as a treatment, preventative or cure for any of the diseases, disorders or abnormal physical states referred to in Schedule A.

The Act broadly defines "advertisement" to be "any representation by any means whatever for the purpose of promoting directly or indirectly the sale or disposal of any food, drug, cosmetic or device". The current list of Schedule "A" diseases and disorders is reasonably long and includes such common maladies as asthma and obesity. Here is the complete list:[49]

Acute alcoholism	Gangrene
Acute anxiety state	Glaucoma
Acute infectious respiratory syndromes	Haematologic bleeding disorders
Acute, inflammatory and debilitating arthritis	Hepatitis
Acute psychotic conditions	Hypertension
Addiction (except nicotine addiction)	Nausea and vomiting of pregnancy
Appendicitis	Obesity

---

of the day, certainty only exists within the context of the facts of a specific case, after the court has rendered its decision.

[49] *Food and Drugs Act.*

Arteriosclerosis	Rheumatic fever
Asthma	Septicemia
Cancer	Sexually transmitted diseases
Congestive heart failure	Strangulated hernia
Convulsions	Thrombotic and Embolic disorders
Dementia	Thyroid disease
Depression	Ulcer of the gastro-intestinal tract
Diabetes	

In the report of the Standing Committee on Health[50] delivered to the House of Commons in 1998, the purpose of this blanket prohibition was identified as being "to ensure individuals will seek medical attention for serious diseases, to restrict advertising when self-diagnosis and self-treatment is not considered advisable and to limit the possibility of fraudulent claims being made with respect to food and drugs." The committee found these provisions to be unduly restrictive to the detriment of consumers, and recommended that Health Canada investigate whether the prohibition should either be eliminated or amended by more tightly defining and/or removing diseases from Schedule "A."

Notwithstanding the Standing Committee's views, section 3 and Schedule "A" of the *Food and Drugs Act* remains in force today. For Holistic Nutritionists who are otherwise permitted to prescribe treatments in their province, the key difficulty with the Act is the breadth of its definitions, which at first blush appear to restrict the making of any representations or claims (i.e., advertisement) about the curative or preventive value of foods (carrots?) and drugs (which would include Natural Health Products) for any Schedule "A" listed disease even if done in the course of a legitimate nutritional consulting practice.

The good news is that the restriction is not quite this tight.

First, the prohibition relates to product labels and to advertising. Since labels are affixed by manufacturers, the concern for Holistic Nutritionists is with advertising, and the definition of advertising clearly states that the representation must be made for the purpose of promoting the sale or disposal of foods, drugs, etc. As a result, only Holistic Nutritionists who are involved directly or indirectly in retailing foods and supplements can be caught by this prohibition, and then only so far as they are making such representations about the ability of the products to treat, etc. a disease and disorders listed in Schedule "A." Holistic Nutritionists who recommend the

---

[50] Canada. Parliament. House of Commons. Standing Committee on Health. *Natural Health Products: A New Vision*. 36th Parliament, 1st Session. (November, 1998).

consumption of certain foods or Natural Health Products and who are not involved in their sale or receiving a commission from the retailer are not engaged in "advertising" (and therefore will not breach the *Food and Drugs Act*) even if their comments extend to representations about the preventive or curative properties of products in relation to a Schedule "A" disease or disorder.

Second, out of a concern that the prohibition against advertising contained in Section 3 of the *Food and Drugs Act* was too broad and contrary to the best interests of consumers, an exception was introduced into the regulations to permit the advertising of preventive claims (but not curative or treatment claims) about Drugs[51] and Natural Health Products[52]. As a result, even Holistic Nutritionists who are directly involved in retailing Natural Health Products may make representations about their ability to prevent (but not cure or treat) Schedule "A" diseases and disorders. Foods are not specifically mentioned in the regulations because, as previously discussed when defining the word "Drug", a substance that is typically viewed as being a "Food" is regulated under the *Food and Drugs Act* as a "Drug" when a representation is made about preventive or curative properties.

Finally, it is important to note that sections 5(1) and 9(1) of the *Food and Drugs Act* also prohibit, among other things, advertising or selling foods or drugs in a manner that is "false, misleading or deceptive or is likely to create an erroneous impression regarding its character, value, quantity, composition, merit or safety."

Holistic Nutritionists who are otherwise permitted to prescribe treatments for diseases and disorders within their provinces and who are involved in retailing foods, drugs or Natural Health Products to the general public, must be careful not to (1) make any representations about the curative and treatment qualities of the items they are selling in respect of the diseases and disorders listed in Schedule "A" to the *Food and Drugs Act*, or (2) make any false, misleading or deceptive claims about its character, value, quantity, composition, merit or safety.

---

[51] Sections A.01.067 and A.01.068, Food and Drug Regulations (C.R.C., c. 870)
[52] Section 103.2 and 103.3 Natural Health Products Regulations SOR/2003-196

Chapter 5
Pulling It All Together

In this book we have looked at some of the reasons why the provision of health services including nutritional health services is regulated, the different approaches used by the provinces for regulation, specific rules that are in place within each province that impact upon a Holistic Nutrition practice, the meanings of key terms used in these rules, and examples from real cases where people have been charged with unlawful practice of Medicine for providing health services that included nutritional advice. This chapter will build upon this foundation to develop some concrete rules Holistic Nutritionists can look to in managing their practices to stay on the right side of the law.

Choose a Lawful Professional Title

In health services, professional titles matter a great deal. They are seen as the primary means by which a profession identifies itself to the public and by which the public identifies the unique education and expertise of a profession's members. Impersonation of a doctor (i.e., the wrongful use of this professional title) is the most common reason cited by many Colleges of Physicians and Surgeons for an unlawful practice prosecution. In health services, every province has created and enforces lists of professional titles that are reserved for use by members of designated Regulated Health Professions. They do, however, approach this issue differently.

Some provinces, such as Ontario, reserve only a very narrow range of specific titles, such as "Physicians" and "Dietitian." Others have lengthy lists that include English and French versions, short forms and other common variations of a main title. For example, Nova Scotia reserves the following titles for use by Registered Dietitians: "Dietitian" or "Dietician"; "Dietitian-Nutritionist"; "Nutritionist"; "Professional Dietitian" or "Professional Dietician"; "Professional

Dietitian-Nutritionist"; "Professional Nutritionist"; "Diététiste"; "Diététiste-Nutritionniste"; "Diététiste Professionelle"; "Diététicienne"; "Nutritionniste" or the initials "P.Dt." or "Dt.P."

Finally, some provinces, in addition to the foregoing, also maintain a general prohibition against using any title that wrongly implies membership in a Regulated Health Profession. In Quebec, for example if you are not a member of the "Ordre professionnel des diététistes du Québec" you may not "take or use any name, title, or description implying or calculated to lead people to infer that the person is a registered dietitian."

Holistic Nutritionists must know the rules that restrict the use of professional titles within the province in which they practice.

As a rule of thumb, a Holistic Nutritionist may use a professional title if it accurately describes his or her education, professional qualifications and practice, is not reserved for use by a Regulated Health Profession, and is otherwise lawfully available for them to use[53]. Where a professional title is restricted (such as "Nutritionist" in Nova Scotia) the safest approach it to also avoid using all equivalent versions of the title in other languages, and all short forms, abbreviations and common variations. Finally, a Holistic Nutritionist should avoid using any professional title that could reasonably be seen as implying he or she is a member of a Regulated Health Profession.

As for the most common titles to avoid, Holistic Nutritionists in all provinces should avoid using any title associated with the medical professions (e.g., Doctor, Dr., MD., Surgeon, Physician, etc.), Naturopathy (e.g., Naturopath, Naturopathic physician, etc.) and the title "Dietitian," which is reserved for use by Registered Dietitians in all Canadian provinces. In addition, Holistic Nutritionists practising in Alberta, Nova Scotia and Quebec should avoid using the title "Nutritionist" plus, of course, as mentioned above, all common variations, abbreviations, and non-English equivalents.

Avoid Using Medical Terms

Many of the rules dealing with professional titles also prohibit any advertisement or claim that is intended to wrongly indicate an ability to diagnose or treat diseases, or membership in a Regulated Health Profession. Holistic Nutritionists should avoid using terms that are associated with the practice of Medicine and other Regulated Health Professions in their advertising, marketing literature and client documents. For example, terms such as: Registered, Medical, Medicine, Naturopathic, Homeopathic, Patients, Diagnostic, Treatment, and their common

---

[53] For example, the professional designations of the Canadian Association of Natural Nutritional Practitioner may only be used by individuals who are member of this organization in good standing.

variations should be avoided. In general, any phrase that could lead a reasonable person to wrongly believe you are a medical doctor, Dietitian, Naturopath (where this is a Regulated Health Profession) or member of another Regulated Health Profession should be avoided.

One representation that has recently become vogue in the Holistic Nutritionist community and which causes me some concern is the trend towards describing nutritional counsellors as "Orthomolecular Health Practitioners." I assume the goal is to carve out a distinct niche for Holistic Nutritionists that separates them from Dietitians. The possible problem, however, is that it is also a reference to a modality that is closely associated with, and in many circles seen to be an aspect of, the practice of Medicine. The Linus Pauling Institute, which continues the work of Dr. Linus Pauling, who is considered the founder of Othomolecular theory, describes orthomolecular Medicine to be "the preservation of good health and the treatment of disease by varying the concentrations in the human body of substances that are normally present in the body" and states that "Orthomolecular Medicine is not 'alternative'; rather, it should be considered as an adjunct to appropriate conventional Medicine."[54] Note the emphasis on treating diseases— which is part of any standard definition of the practice of Medicine. I believe there is a very real risk that Holistic Nutritionists who promote themselves under the Orthomolecular banner could be found to be representing that they are authorized to perform the services of a Medical Doctor.

Avoid Diagnosing Diseases and Disorders

Every province with the exception of Alberta either directly or indirectly[55] reserves the act of diagnosing diseases and disorders to specific regulated health professions. This means Holistic Nutritionists in every province other than Alberta must be careful not to render a diagnosis. This can be difficult. There is nothing more natural, and indeed, more intuitive perhaps, when dealing with clients than inquiring into their health history and complaints. How can this be done safely? Here are some suggestions:

- Restrict enquiries and activities to evaluating degrees of health. Medicine approaches health from the perspective of identifying and curing diseases. Where there are no diseases or abnormal conditions, health is considered to be present. By contrast, Holistic Nutritionists seek to investigate and enhance health. The act of identifying dietary and nutritional habits that can be changed to improve overall health does not constitute diagnosing diseases and disorders.

---

[54] Linus Pauling Institute [online]. [Cited January 27, 2011.] <http://lpi.oregonstate.edu/>.
[55] I consider rendering a diagnosis to be indirectly restricted in any province where the practice of medicine is restricted, as it is clear from case law that the practice of medicine includes diagnosing human diseases and conditions.

- Avoid reaching conclusions based on symptomology. If a disease or disorder is suspected, the client should be told of this suspicion and told to consult a doctor. Never render a verdict or make a conclusion about a client's health. Do not say "You have cancer" or "low blood sugar" or "an iron deficiency." A diagnosis is a conclusion about health and is not something Holistic Nutritionists are typically trained to do.

- When reporting a suspected disease or disorder to a client, put it in writing so there is clear evidence that the client was (1) notified of a suspicion, (2) informed a suspicion is not a diagnosis or conclusion about the state of his or her health, and (3) directed to consult a doctor.

- Do not diagnose symptoms. Do not link symptoms to diseases.

- Emphasize educating clients about good nutrition. Empower clients to make their own conclusions about their health.

- Be aware of the enforcement practices of regulators and their threshold for enforcement.

- Have clients list all known diseases and disorders on their in-take forms. If a client reveals a disease or disorder, one is not making a diagnosis.

- Do not order blood and other medical diagnostic tests or collect specimens from the human body.

- Never second-guess a diagnosis made by a doctor or other Regulated Health Professional. If an error is suspected, encourage the client to obtain a second opinion from another qualified practitioner.

- Whenever possible, practice in conjunction with a medical doctor or naturopath or a member of another appropriate Regulated Health Profession in your province.

Holistic Nutritionists who practice in Alberta are permitted to make a diagnosis. However, as this is not a skill Holistic Nutritionists are typically trained to perform, one should venture down this path very carefully, and only if properly trained. Performing a diagnosis in Alberta may be legal, but one can still cause great harm if wrong and be sued by a client for malpractice if negligent.

Avoid Treating Diseases and Disorders if Practising Outside Alberta and Ontario.

Different provinces take different positions on the treatment of diseases. At the time this is being written, Holistic Nutritionists who practice within British Columbia[56], Manitoba[57], New Brunswick, Newfoundland and Labrador, Nova Scotia, Prince Edward Island, Quebec and Saskatchewan are either directly or indirectly[58] prohibited from prescribing treatments for diseases and disorders.

Holistic Nutritionists who practice within Alberta and Ontario may prescribe treatments for diseases and disorders, provided they do so safely, do not perform a Restricted Activity, and comply with the provisions of the *Food and Drugs Act*, including its prohibition against advertising cures and treatments for diseases and disorders listed in Schedule "A" of the Act.

For Holistic Nutritionists who practice within a province where prescribing a treatment is restricted, what can they do? How does one assist clients to improve health, but not be seen to be prescribing treatment? Here are some suggestions:

- Do not claim to "treat" or manage a disease or disorder and do not promise to cure or improve a known health condition. Food and nutritional supplements do not cure diseases or conditions; they strengthen the body and enhance the body's ability to maximize its own health.

- Do not prescribe products, or dietary changes to address a known health condition, unless doing so under the supervision of a Regulated Health Professional, where such joint practices are lawful. The threshold for what constitutes prescribing a treatment is very low. Any attempt to "manage" a recognized disease or disorder, through any means, constitutes treatment, regardless of how safe or common the remedies prescribed.

- Do not second-guess a treatment prescribed by a doctor or other Regulated Health Professional. If an error is suspected, encourage the client to obtain a second opinion from another qualified practitioner.

---

[56] Once the Restricted Activities are enacted and assuming there are no changes from the draft currently being proposed, the making of a diagnosis will be restricted, but not prescribing a treatment, unless doing so involves another procedure which is restricted.
[57] After The Regulated Health Professions Act comes into force the making of a diagnosis will be restricted, but not prescribing a treatment, unless doing so involves another procedure which is restricted.
[58] I consider prescribing a treatment to be indirectly restricted in any province where the practice of Medicine is restricted, as it is clear from case law that the practice of Medicine includes treating human diseases and disorders.

- Always instruct clients to consult a licensed Physician or Naturopath (where Naturopathy is a Regulated Health Profession) about any suspected disease or disorders.

- Keep a record of a client's doctor and the advice the doctor has provided.

- Emphasize educating clients about good nutrition. This may be done without restriction in all provinces.

- Be aware of the enforcement practices of regulators and their threshold for enforcement.

- If possible, practice in conjunction with a Medical Doctor or Naturopath or a member of another appropriate Regulated Health Profession.

- Do not prescribe drugs and medications. This is an aspect of practising Medicine, or a Restricted Activity, in all Canadian provinces.

- Do not prescribe Homeopathic remedies. Regardless of whether they are considered drugs, they are substances that are designed to treat diseases and disorders.

- Recommend only foods or Health Canada approved Natural Health Products.[59] Licensed products can be identified by an eight digit product licence number beginning with the letters "NPN" or "DIN-HM".[60] Exempt products can be identified by a product code beginning with the letters "EN."

- Holistic Nutritionists who sell foods, drugs or Natural Health Products must comply with the provisions of the *Food and Drugs Act* which permits the making of preventive claims about the products being sold, but not the making of curative or treatment claims, so far as they relate to diseases and disorders listed in Schedule "A" of the Act.

- Holistic Nutritionists who manufacture their own Natural Health Products, must comply with the manufacturing and licensing provisions of the Natural Health Product Regulations under the *Food and Drugs Act*, as well as any applicable provincial rules relating to food and/or drug manufacturing handling and distribution.

---

[59] Commencing February 2011 it is illegal in Canada to sell a Natural Health Product unless that product holds a Natural Health Product Licence, or exemption.

[60] The DIN-HM designation applies to homeopathic remedies.

Know the Practice Restrictions That Apply Within Your Province

As mentioned may times throughout this book, the provision of health services is regulated provincially. What is lawful in one province may not be lawful in another. Holistic Nutritionists must know the rules that exist within the province in which they practise and avoid relying upon chat groups and discussion forums for guidance.

Holistic Nutritionists who practise in Alberta, Ontario or Quebec must know and avoid all Restricted Activities within their province. Holistic Nutritionists practising in the other provinces must avoid any activity that is included within the scope of the practice of Medicine. This is crucial because "practice of Medicine" is broadly defined by the Courts, and as we have seen, includes among many other activities, diagnosing and prescribing nutritional treatments for diseases and disorders.

Of particular relevance for Holistic Nutritionists are acts and procedures that relate to nutrition and dietary management, because these are closest in nature to what Holistic Nutritionists do. For example, in Quebec common sense may tell one that "providing pregnancy care and conducting deliveries" are Restricted Activities. However, a Holistic Nutritionist practising in Quebec must also be aware that only a member of the Ordre professionnel des diététistes du Québec (or another Regulated Health Plan that is similarly authorized) may "(a) determine a nutritional plan, including the appropriate feeding route, where an individual prescription indicates that nutrition is a determining factor in the treatment of illness; and (b) monitor the nutritional status of persons whose nutritional treatment plan has been determined." Similarly, Holistic Nutritionists practising in British Columbia should be aware that only Registered Dietitians may "design, compound or dispense therapeutic diets if nutrition is administered through enteral means."

Holistic Nutritionists practising within the provinces of New Brunswick, Nova Scotia and Manitoba need to exercise particular caution. In New Brunswick the *Dietitians Act* restricts virtually all nutritional counselling to registered Dietitians and other similarly authorized Regulated Health Professions. This will also be the state of affairs in Nova Scotia once its new *Dietitians Act* is proclaimed into force. In Manitoba, it is arguable that that nutritional counselling is presently reserved for registered Naturopaths, at least until this province's new *Health Professions Act* comes into force.

In all cases, readers should refer back to the rules in place in within the province in which they practise for a complete list of what may and may not be done.

Know Your Regulator

From my discussions with several of the provincial Colleges of Physicians and Surgeons, it is clear that enforcement is viewed differently in different provinces. The province of Quebec, for example, is known for strictly enforcing its prohibition against unlawfully diagnosing and prescribing treatment and frequently proceeds against naturopaths (naturopathy is not a Regulated Health Profession in Quebec) and others who provide such advice. This province has a strong consumer protection bias in favour of its Regulated Health Professions. By contrast, the College of Physicians and Surgeons of Saskatchewan maintains an official policy in favour of consumer choice, and informed me that it restricts its enforcement activities to situations of fraud (e.g., where a health service provider impersonates a doctor) and physical harm. The consequence of these two different philosophies is that even though diagnosing and prescribing treatment is directly or indirectly restricted in both provinces, several people are prosecuted each year in Quebec and it has been several years since anyone has been prosecuted in Saskatchewan.

It is crucially important for Holistic Nutritionists to be aware of the enforcement practices within their province.

If it does not make sense to you that provinces enforce their laws differently, consider how speeding is enforced on our highways. If the maximum posted limit is 100 km/hr, travelling at 101 km/hr is illegal and should result in a fine. However, because it is not practical for police to enforce such minor speed violations, they don't begin issuing tickets until a greater violation has occurred, perhaps ten, fifteen or even twenty km/hr over the posted limit. The point at which the police begin to enforce the speed limit depends upon their view of public safety and the practicality of enforcement. On a straight stretch of highway where all the cars are exceeding the posted limit, speeding by five or ten km/hr will likely be ignored. If however, one is passing car after car on a busy section of road or near a school, the same five or ten km/hr infraction may lead to a ticket. The bottom line is that discretion is being used to determine when to enforce the law.

Enforcement practices with respect to health services work in a similar manner. In some provinces regulators recognize different people are attracted to different health modalities and embrace the idea that individuals should be entitled to choose their own health care provider, no matter how unconventional. They enforce their laws accordingly and tend to proceed only in egregious cases of fraud or risky, invasive procedures. Other provinces take a more paternalistic approach and believe it is the regulator's job to determine which modalities are valid and the level of training required for practitioners. These provinces tend to favour Regulated Health Professions over all others and they enforce their laws accordingly.

Of course, over time, the laws themselves should change to reflect these underlying viewpoints. But this takes time, political will and money. In the meantime, accommodation is often made through adjusting enforcement practices.

Readers can learn about the enforcement practices within the province in which they practice by contacting the Colleges of Physicians and Surgeons, Naturopathy and Dietitians. In some provinces, one or more of these bodies are directly responsible for enforcement, while in others they only provide support to the Crown. In either case, they can usually help one better understand how the law is interpreted and enforced, or provide a referral to someone who can.

I often find non-lawyers are hesitant to contact regulators, believing they will put themselves on a watch list if they do. If this is a concern, do not provide your name, or if asked, advise the regulator that you are calling on a no-names basis. Regulators usually have a public education mandate and are more than willing to offer help. It is also important to understand that enforcement practices can change at any time, usually without announcement. So check back frequently.

Keep Current

Laws change. What is lawful today may not be lawful tomorrow. No matter where one lives in Canada, a good continuing education program includes being aware of the changes to the laws that govern health services.

As we have seen in this book, the provinces of British Columbia and Manitoba are both in the process of changing the way they regulate health services. Holistic Nutritionists practising in British Columbia should watch for the introduction of Restricted Activities in that province. Similarly, those practising in Manitoba should watch for the repeal of the existing health regulation rules and the proclamation into force of the *Regulated Health Professions Act* and the changes this will introduce. Finally, Holistic Nutritionists practising in Nova Scotia must watch and plan for the coming into force of the new *Dietitians Act*. Once in effect, this Act will make it virtually impossible for a Holistic Nutritionist to lawfully provide any type of services to clients.

Practise Within the Scope of Your Training

This book has focused on some of the major rules imposed by the various governments of Canada that regulate, in a meaningful way, the practices of Holistic Nutritionists. In addition to complying with the law, however, Holistic Nutritionists must also be careful to practise within the boundaries of their skill and education. A failure to do so can result in harm to clients (Remember the Kishes, who prescribed internal and external treatments of hydrogen peroxide as a cure for lung cancer?), lead to law suits for malpractice (i.e., professional negligence) and even prosecution for fraud under the *Criminal Code* if one's actions involve knowingly making false claims or misrepresenting skill and training or professional accreditation. This principle should also be carried through to one's marketing literature and client materials. Remember, many provinces not only restrict what one can do, but also what one can say about what does. Never misrepresent or over-promise what can be achieved for clients.

Use Appropriate Forms and Waivers

As we saw under the discussions of "practice of Medicine," "diagnosis" and "treatment" in the last chapter, it really doesn't matter whether one intended to engage in a restricted practice or activity; all that really matters is one's actions. Using correct forms, however, can establish a client's expectations and provide evidence about the content and nature of advice. This can be particularly important in provinces where making a diagnosis is restricted (i.e., all provinces other than Alberta) and an assessment of a client leads one to suspect the presence of a disease or disorder, or the client is seeking treatment (where this may lawfully be done) for a disease or disorder that has been self-diagnosed, or diagnosed by a doctor.

A good in-take form (or forms) should cover the following points[61] (I have also included a sample assumption of risk and release of liability form at the end of this chapter):

- You are trained in the body's nutritional needs and you are not a licensed Physician Naturopath or Dietitian.

- You are relying upon the truth and accuracy of all information provided to you by the client, including medical history and the presence or absences of diseases, disorders, etc.

- You do not diagnose [in all provinces except Alberta] or treat [all provinces except Alberta, and Ontario] diseases or disorders.

- If you suspect a client suffers from a disease or disorder, the client will be notified. However, this should not be seen as a diagnosis or relied upon in any way, and a medical doctor or other appropriate health professional should be consulted.

- The purpose of nutritional counselling is to improve the body's immune system and overall vitality. Dietary changes and other recommendations should not be seen as, or relied upon for, treating diseases or disorder [all provinces except Alberta and Ontario].

---

[61] It is also important to remember that your collection, storage, use and release of client information must comply with privacy and collection of personal information laws in effect in your province, such as Ontario's *Personal Health Information Protection Act*, and the federal government's *Personal Information Protection and Electronic Documents Act*.

- If a client notifies you of a disease, disorder for which they are seeking nutritional treatment, you are relying without independent verification, upon this diagnosis. If they have not done so, they should have it verified by a medical doctor or other appropriate health professional. [Alberta and Ontario only.]

Join a Good Professional Association

As mentioned at the beginning of the book, Holistic Nutritionists, unlike Registered Dietitians, Medical Doctors, and in some provinces Naturopaths, are not members of a Regulated Health Profession. This means there is no governing body overseeing the profession to whom Holistic Nutritionists are accountable and to whom the public can appeal when they have questions or complaints.

The benefit of this is that Holistic Nutritionists are free to structure their practices and provide advice any way they see fit, provided they do not perform a procedure that is restricted in their province and/or engage in a restricted professional practice, and otherwise comply with laws of general application. The problem with this situation, however, is that there are no guidelines establishing what it means to be a Holistic Nutritionist and anyone, regardless of education or qualifications, can claim to practice in this area, as long as they do not fraudulently misrepresent their credentials, and, of course, otherwise comply with the law. This makes it difficult for properly trained ethical Holistic Nutritionists to stand out, and for the public to know the difference.

In response to this situation, several associations have formed over the years to assist Holistic Nutritionists with their practices and to provide the public with a means of skill validation and accountability. The decision of which association is best for you is a personal one. In the interest of full disclosure, I want to point out right now that I am a director of one of these associations—the Canadian Association of Natural Nutritional Practitioners (CANNP). I believe it does the best job representing the interests of its Holistic Nutritionists, and, naturally, favour it over the others. Regardless of this, however, if you are deciding among associations, I have the following recommendations:

- Nutritionist associations are not governing bodies and do not confer upon their members the right to practice as a Holistic Nutritionist.

- Nutritionist associations exist to serve their members. The only reason to join one is to take advantage of the benefits offered to members.

- Confirm the association is a non-profit corporation. A non-profit corporation is a corporation that has members, not shareholders, and which is required by law to use the money it collects from membership fees, etc. to fulfill its mandate. It is not permitted to generate a profit. If an association does not permit its members to elect the association's board of directors, ask questions. Odds are the association is not a "non-profit."

- Make sure the association has comprehensive professional guidelines and rules of practice. In a legal action for malpractice, compliance with professional standards and practices is an available defense. An association's professional guidelines and rules of practice can help ensure their members practise in accordance with professional standards, and serve as evidence that they did.

- There is no legal requirement compelling Holistic Nutritionists to maintain practice liability insurance. Having such insurance is, however, typically required as a condition of membership in a Nutritionist association for two reasons: (1) it protects the member by making money available in the event of a legal action for malpractice, and (2) it protects the member's client by ensuring funds are available for damages in the event they are successful in a legal action for malpractice.

- Make sure the association responds to questions and assists with mentoring. These are the services that help Holistic Nutritionists avoid making professional practice and business mistakes.

Relax and Enjoy What You Do

Holistic Nutritionists provide invaluable services to the public. Their goal is to make people healthy. What can be better than this? Yes, there are many rules that restrict what can be done. But with the exception of New Brunswick[62] where a conventional Holistic Nutritionist's practice contravenes the exclusive practice area of Dietitians, and possibly Manitoba where the *Naturopathic Act* may be a problem (at least until Manitoba's *Health Professions Act* comes into force), these restrictions exist to either ensure the public knows the professional background and expertise of their health service providers (restrictions relating to professional titles, advertising and representation), or to ensure high-risk procedures and the diagnosis and treatment of diseases and conditions are performed by those who have requisite training.

The truth of the matter is that thousands of Holistic Nutritionists provide their services to the public every day, and based upon the legal research I completed, and the anecdotal evidence I collected from the Colleges of Physicians and Surgeon, Colleges of Dietitians and police forces I contacted while researching this book, actions against nutritional advisors are for the most part rare and primarily relate to egregious situations of practising Medicine (e.g., the Kishes),

---

[62] Nova Scotia will also be in this group, once its new *Dietitians Act* is proclaimed.

unlawful prescription of treatments, and incidences of fraud, where individuals wrongfully represent themselves to the public as Doctors, or the possessors of miracle cures. In short, the fraudsters and quacks we briefly looked at in the first chapter who prey upon the unsuspecting public.

Appendix 1
Assumption of Risk and Release of Liability
For Nutrition Counselling Services

The Assumption of Risk and Release of Liability contains two parts.

The first part deals with the client's assumption of risk. This part of the form is designed to minimize liability by ensuring a client receives notice of certain key facts about the practice of Holistic Nutrition and its limitations. In provinces where use of the title "Nutritionist" is restricted, substitute an acceptable title such as "Advisor" or "Counsellor." References to Naturopaths should be included only in provinces where Naturopaths are a Regulated Health Profession. Reference to treatment can be omitted in the provinces in which a Holistic Nutritionist is permitted to provide treatments. In provinces where Holistic Nutritionists are permitted to treat clients, the alternative version of paragraph 5 should be used.

The second part of this form is a release of liability. The purpose of this release is to minimize liability by having the client release the practitioner from any liability for any negative consequences that may result from the counselling service.

In relying upon this form the following factors must be taken into account:

- This form is provided to illustrate the types of issues an Assumption of Risk and Release of Liability form may deal with.

- The laws of the provinces of Canada differ. All or part of this form may not be enforceable within a particular province.

- Prior to relying upon this form, it should be reviewed by a lawyer licensed to practise in the province within which it is to be used.

- Clients must be of legal age and sound mind when signing a form of this type. Clients should be encouraged to carefully read, ask questions, and if requested, consult a lawyer about any documents they are asked to sign. Never intimidate or coerce a client into signing a form of this type.

Assumption of Risk and Release of Liability
For Nutrition Counselling Services

TO: [insert name of Holistic Nutritionist] (the "Nutritionist[63]")

DATE: [insert date]

RE: Nutrition Counselling Services

The undersigned, _____, hereby acknowledges and agrees as follows:

1. The purpose of nutrition counselling is to improve the overall health, vitality and well-being of the body through nutritional education and the use of natural foods and non-medicinal nutritional supplements. The [Nutritionist] does not diagnose [or treat][64] diseases, disorders or conditions.

2. The [Nutritionist] is not a licensed Dietitian, [Naturopath][65] or Physician.

3. As part of the Nutrition Counselling Services, I may be asked to provide information concerning my physical habits, medical history, moods, energy levels, likes and dislikes, lifestyle and diet. This information is collected to enable the Nutritionist to (i) assess my knowledge of nutrition, (ii) educate me about the benefits of sound nutritional practices, and (iii) recommend dietary changes to improve my general health, vitality and overall well-being. The [Nutritionist] will hold this information in confidence and will not release or disclose this information to any other person, without my prior consent, except as required by applicable law.

4. If the [Nutritionist] suspects the existence of a disease, disorder or condition, I will be informed of this suspicion. However, I acknowledge this is not a diagnosis or conclusion about the state of my health and that I am directed to promptly consult a licensed Physician [or Naturopath] about any suspected problems.

5. Dietary changes and nutritional supplements suggested by the [Nutritionist] are intended to improve the general health, vitality and well-being of my body and are not recommended for the purposes of treating diseases, disorders or conditions. I am not to alter or discontinue treatments prescribed by a licensed [Naturopath], Physician or other

---

[63] In provinces where use of the title "Nutritionist" is restricted, substitute an acceptable title such as "Advisor" or "Counsellor."

[64] Reference to treatment can be omitted in the provinces in which a Holistic Nutritionist is permitted to provide treatments.

[65] Include references to Naturopaths only in provinces where Naturopaths are a Regulated Health Profession.

licensed health professional without consulting the individual who prescribed the treatment.

– Alternate paragraph 5 –

[IN PROVINCES IN WHICH A HOLISTIC NUTRITIONIST IS PERMITTED TO PROVIDE TREATMENT, THE FOLLOWING CAN BE SUBSTITUTED FOR PARAGRAPH 5 ABOVE] Should I request the [Nutritionist] to recommend dietary changes and/or nutritional supplements to enhance my body's natural ability to resist and/or overcome a known disease, disorder or condition, it is my responsibility to disclose the nature of the disease, disorder or condition and all other relevant details to the [Nutritionist]. If I have not previously consulted a licensed Physician [or Naturopath] about the disease, disorder or condition, I acknowledge that I am directed to promptly do so. I am not to alter or discontinue treatments prescribed by a licensed [Naturopath], Physician or other licensed health professional without consulting the individual who prescribed the treatment.

6. In providing Nutrition Counselling Services to me, the [Nutritionist] is relying upon the truth, accuracy and completeness of all information I have provided to him/her. Any recommendations I follow for changes in diet, including the use of nutritional supplements, are entirely my responsibility.

In consideration of my participation in the Nutrition Counselling Services, I hereby accept all risk to my health, including injury or death that may result from such participation and I hereby release the [Nutritionist], on my behalf and on behalf of my personal representatives, estate, heirs, next of kin and assigns from any and all costs, claims, causes of action and damages arising from any and all illness or injury to my person, including my death, that may result from or occur as a result of my participation in the Nutrition Counselling Services, whether caused by negligence or otherwise.

I HAVE CAREFULLY READ THIS AGREEMENT AND UNDERSTAND IT TO BE A FULL AND FULL AND FINAL RELEASE OF ALL COSTS, CLAIMS, CAUSES OF ACTION AND DAMAGES OF ANY KIND ARISING FROM OR IN CONNECTION WITH THE NUTRITION COUNSELLING SERVICES.

_____   _____
Client Signature   Date

Made in the USA
Charleston, SC
09 June 2013